Janáček and Brod

Max Brod at 30, from a previously unpublished photograph (courtesy of Francis Sterne).

Janáček and Brod

Charles Susskind

Foreword by Sir Charles Mackerras

YALE UNIVERSITY PRESS
New Haven and London

Designed by Margaret E.B. Joyner
and set in Times Roman with Deepdene type
by Brevis Press.
Printed in the United States of America
by Halliday Lithograph.

Library of Congress Cataloging in Publication Data

Susskind, Charles.
  Janáček and Brod.

  Bibliography: p.
  Includes index.
  1. Janáček, Leoš, 1854–1928—Friends and associates.
2. Brod, Max, 1884–1968—Friends and associates.
3. Composers—Czechoslovakia—Biography. 4. Authors,
Austrian—20th century—Biography. I. Title.
ML410.J18S95 1985   780'.92'4 [B]   85–8227
ISBN 0–300–03420–2 (alk. paper)

The paper in this book meets the guidelines for permanence
and durability of the Committee on Production Guidelines
for Book Longevity of the Council on Library Resources.

10 9 8 7 6 5 4 3 2 1

To the memory of

WALTER SUSSKIND

(1913–1980)

Contents

ILLUSTRATIONS

Foreword

Sir Charles Mackerras

When one considers the present-day reputation of Janáček as one of the greatest opera composers of the twentieth century, it hardly seems credible that not so long ago he was looked down upon as a rather quirky, "folksy" provincial, whose main work centered around an unpronounceable town in the middle of Czechoslovakia. From that sleepy town of Brno was developed the career of Moravia's greatest artistic son; and at least two of his operas have brought the moral and cultural mores of that colorful and beautiful part of Europe to the whole world, as far removed from its original background as (for example) California and Australia.

The present book is a reminder to Janáček enthusiasts that his fame was not easily won. Janáček had a tremendous struggle to get his first important opera, *Jenufa,* performed in Prague, which, although not yet the capital of the new Czechoslovakia, was at least the fountainhead of culture in the Czech language. But he found a strong champion from an unexpected source. The Jewish German-speaking litterateur Max Brod became so possessed by Janáček's work that he determined it should be performed in Vienna, then still the capital of the Hapsburg empire, and succeeded in helping Janáček to that end, not only by his recommendations but by actually translating his operas into German.

In this year of 1984, the centenary of the birth of Max Brod, it is appropriate to be reminded not only of Brod's services to Czech literature through his support of such widely diverse authors as Kafka and Hašek, but also that Janáček could never have achieved anything more than a local provincial reputation without Brod's enthusiastic propagation of his work.

Charles Susskind captures exactly the contrast between the artistic milieu of the Jewish intelligentsia in Prague, as represented by Brod, and the passionate Slavism of the nature-loving pantheist Janáček. He also emphasizes a third dimension: that even after the creation of the Czechoslovak republic, Vienna still remained the artistic capital of Central Europe. It was the Viennese first performance in Brod's German translation that really put *Jenufa* on the map, from where, still in Brod's translation, it spread over Europe and as far away as the New York Met. (It is also interesting to note that many Austrians associated with the progress of *Jenufa* had Germanized Czech names: Hertzka, von Wymetal, Jeritza.)

Brod's translations provided the channel for the international recognition of Janáček's operas, because most of the important opera houses between the two world wars were German. The interest shown in Janáček's works by famous German conductors such as Otto Klemperer, Erich Kleiber, and Bruno Walter gave them a certain cachet. It is safe to say that if the first German translations of Janáček's operas had been of lower quality, the operas themselves would not have attained such wide recognition. And Brod was also Janáček's first biographer.

Charles Susskind describes in fascinating detail the genesis of most of Janáček's important works and Brod's influence on them. Particularly interesting are the many extracts from the correspondence between the two artists, published here for the first time in English. (Although Brod knew Czech perfectly, he always wrote Janáček in German and Janáček would reply in Czech!) The correspondence shows how the two men collaborated and how the cosmopolitan Brod often suggested major changes in the dramatic content of the operas that Janáček, with his native dramatic instinct, usually refused to accept.

Other items of interest brought out in the narrative are the cooling off in the friendship between Janáček and his great supporter Marie Calma, when she was not chosen to sing the role of Jenufa in the Prague première; and also, by contrast, the growth of the intimate liaison between the composer and Gabriela Horvátová, the first Prague Kostelnička. Readers familiar with operatic politics and finance may find the excuses of the theater directors for *not* putting on *Jenufa* edifying, also the fact that both the Prague and Viennese premières could take place while the First World War was at its height.

Charles Susskind is in an ideal position to evoke the Central European milieu of the early days of the first Czechoslovak republic: not only does he come from the same background, he is the brother of the famous Czech-born conductor Walter Susskind. Expatriate Czech musicians such as Susskind, Firkušný, and Rafael Kubelík did much to bring the music of Janáček and other Czech composers to the attention of the wider world (particularly America), without which the later generation of Janáček interpreters, like myself, could never have succeeded.

The appearance of this book is most timely, lest the new wave of German translations of Janáček's operas and the new approach to his music should sweep away the remembrance of his first great collaborator, propagator, and biographer.

My preface ends with the same words of Firkušný's as Susskind's book: "Without Max Brod, Leoš Janáček's world reputation would not have arrived for many more years." Perhaps never.

Brod

He was not a commanding figure: a short, bespectacled gnome of a man, almost a hunchback, whom a childhood kyphosis had left with a slight curvature of the spine and one shoulder permanently lower than the other. Yet he made an unforgettable impression on all who came within his sphere. Despite his deformity, he had a legendary success with women. He was a novelist, poet, critic, composer—yet keenly aware of his limitations and ever ready to champion neglected contemporaries whose talent he recognized as greater than his own. He brought at least three truly major talents to the world's attention, against odds that would have daunted a less determined man, by a single-mindedness that overcame indifference and obscurity imposed by the accidents of politics and geography. He was instrumental in turning the last of the three, his longtime friend Franz Kafka, into one of the luminaries of world literature, an international star of such brilliance that its glow tends to put its discoverer altogether in the shade, so that he is best known as Kafka's literary executor and biographer—a latter-day Boswell to Kafka's Johnson. The two earlier instances are less familiar. One was Jaroslav Hašek, author of *The Good Soldier Švejk* (Schwejk), whom he was the first to recognize as a humorist of the top rank and about whom he said in an early review that future generations might not find comparison with Cervantes and Rabelais too farfetched. It was this review that led to the first translation (into German, by Grete Reiner) and to Brod's own dramatization of that quintessential antiwar novel, which remains the most translated work of Czech literature. The other instance was Leoš Janáček.

Max Brod was born in Prague in 1884, at a time when the city was a bubbling cauldron of political, nationalist, and artistic polemics that continued until his departure in 1939, well after the town had ceased to be a provincial center of the moribund Austro-Hungarian Empire and had become the exuberant capital of Tomáš Masaryk's short-lived Czechoslovak republic. In his 1960 autobiography, *Ein streitbares Leben* (A Contentious Life), Brod sought to justify its title by characterizing himself as a "polemicist against my will" and said that the many controversies in which he had become embroiled were not so much his own doing as the fault of his hometown: it was a place in which polemics went on not merely among individuals but among the three contending nationalities as well. There was the Czech majority, the German minority, and the Jewish minority within that minority; and the situation was complicated by the lack of consensus about whether the Jews were a nation or a religion or both, and by their increasing tendency to identify with the Czechs.

But not the writers among them. They might be fluent in Czech (a Slav language related to Russian), but their mother tongue and education and literary heritage were those of the German-speaking ruling class, and secondarily French. The Czech language was only just recovering from three centuries of neglect under the Hapsburgs; it was spoken by a few million people in Bohemia, Moravia, and parts of Silesia—whereas German was spoken throughout Austria proper, Germany, and most of Switzerland, and read by educated people in many of the lands that bordered on this region. The potential audience for a literary work in German numbered ten times the total of Czech readers, and the access to readers of other world languages through translations was incomparably greater. To this day, the only Czech writers besides Hašek to achieve world reputations are Karel Čapek, who was a dramatist as well as a novelist and the author of a hit play, *R.U.R.*; and Milan Kundera, who now lives in France. (Each has a place in our story.) The other Bohemian writers known to the world—Meyrink, Rilke, Kafka, Werfel, Brod himself—all wrote in German. The Jews among

Max Brod. Cartoon by Lucian Bernhard.

them had another reason to stick with the language of the Hapsburgs: had not the Emperor Josef II, Mozart's patron, freed
them from the ghetto a century before? It was by no means clear
that their Czech neighbors, if they ever got the upper hand,
would be equally tolerant of such a minority, especially in view
of its identification with the hated Austrian rulers. When that
moment arrived, in 1918, Max Brod found himself in the fore-
front of those who sought to persuade the new regime of the
importance of a tolerant policy toward *all* minorities, and actually elicited a cabled promise from Tomáš Masaryk (who was
then in America) to Brod to safeguard the rights and security of
the new republic's Jewish citizens. (Their number had been
greatly augmented by the accession of two former Hungarian
provinces, Slovakia and Ruthenia.)

Young Max attended German schools: five years of primary
and eight years of secondary school, the classical *Gymnasium*
whose curriculum included eight years of Latin and five years of
Greek, in addition to enough mathematics and science to enable
its graduates to opt for careers in medicine or science as well as
law, divinity, or "philology"—the arts and humanities. (Future
engineers and architects went to a seven-year *Realschule* and
learned modern languages and subjects such as descriptive ge-
ometry; and there was also an intermediate choice, the *Realgym-
nasium,* where science and one classical and one modern
language were taught.) After secondary came higher education,
in the same two categories: university and *Technik* (engineering
college), both in two versions, Czech and German. The duality
in language extended to many other institutions. Art and music
schools, opera, theater, bookstores, even glee clubs and civic
organizations all existed in twin editions, much as they still do
in Brussels or Montreal. Max Brod enrolled at the German university and in due course earned a law degree, which qualified
him for an excruciatingly boring job in the legal department of
the general post office. He spent the war of 1914–1918 and some
time afterward there, until he found that he could make his way
by belles lettres and journalism. Till then, like many another
writer before and after, he preferred to pursue the muses without
relying on them for a living.

Brod's career was so long and so eventful—he lived into the

last third of the twentieth century and died in his eighty-fifth year in 1968, furiously active to the last—that one finds it difficult to remember that he was already thirty when the war broke out in 1914. By then he had published countless short stories, half a dozen novels, plays, translations (from Latin—the poems of Catullus—and from French and Czech), and several books of poetry. His earliest verses were collected in a slim volume called *Der Weg des Verliebten* (The Enamored's Way), published in Berlin in 1907, which earned the approbation of Rilke. The reception of his 1909 novella *Ein tschechisches Dienstmädchen* (A Czech Maidservant) was a foretaste of the witches' brew of political and other nonliterary opinion and criticism that might be the lot of any Central European writer who dared to make the complexities of a multinational society his subject.

Brod's family was moderately affluent but not rich. When the childhood disease that nearly crippled him required special treatment and a prolonged stay in a foreign sanatorium (the practical orthopedist Friedrich von Hessing's Bavarian clinic), his father had to eke out his bank officer's salary by moonlighting as an accountant. Yet the family could afford an annual seaside holiday, at Misdroy on the Baltic Sea. Brod and his mother, sister, and brother undertook the lengthy rail journey at the start of each summer, accompanied by a maidservant. His father, whose vacation from the bank was shorter, came somewhat later. The mother was the stronger personality. Later, she grew increasingly eccentric and ultimately had to be placed in a nursing home. The gradual worsening of her mental fitness showed up first in the endless warfare with the maids, who seldom lasted long. One of them ended by killing herself while in the family's service. The police investigation that followed uncovered an unhappy love affair, but ugly rumors kept circulating around the neighborhood, and an opportunistic communist ward heeler arranged a local demonstration against the oppressive employer. The ever-changing parade of maids was grist for the young author's mill. *Ein tschechisches Dienstmädchen* is the story of a young Viennese, William Schurhaft, who finds a modest job in a business in Prague and lives there in double isolation: as an inexperienced and inept son of the bourgeoisie whose ideas of life are quite abstract, and as a German-speaking man from the imperial capital among the Czech provincials. He is completely outside the mainstream of the life that goes on around him—until he falls in love with a Czech maidservant. The affair leads him into real life; when it ends, he slides back into despair and sterile phantasmagoria.

The reviews were mixed, with attacks from several quarters. The Czech writer Růžena Jesenská (an aunt of Kafka's later great love Milena Jesenská) saw in the little book an affront to the Czech nation, here personified as a subservient class whose only attributes were the physical. The sympathetic and understanding way in which the Czechs were portrayed, with their many talents and graces, was taken for granted. Yet that was precisely what caught the eye of the German critics, who perceived their landsmen as locked in a deadly struggle against an oppressive Czech majority and who equated empathy with high treason. Nor was that all. To Brod's great bewilderment, he was attacked by Jewish critics as well. Was not William Schurhaft, his hero, the very model of the artificial, rootless *type* of big-city Jew, his cosmopolitanism affirmed by his unusual English first name? And did the author believe that national questions could be resolved in bed? That was scarcely what Brod had intended—and yet he had to admit to himself that he had unconsciously produced an archetype.

Despite such setbacks, Brod had clearly made a name for himself before he was twenty-five, with a Berlin publisher and a respectable oeuvre in both poetry and prose. His acquaintance with Franz Kafka dated back to 1902; although both had attended the same Catholic primary school, staffed by the selfless fathers of the Piarist order, Franz was a year ahead, and the two boys never met until both were law students, still an academic year apart. Their first common interest was philosophy, not literature. (Brod admired Schopenhauer extravagantly and despised Nietzsche; Kafka sought to talk his new friend out of such fanatically extreme views.) In any case, although he was the younger of the two, Brod was to become an established writer long before anyone had ever heard of Kafka. But in the same year that Brod published his controversial novella, he became aware of a new and shining poetic talent, a youth who was then in his last year at the Gymnasium and whose unpublished verses really took one's breath away. With characteristic generosity and boundless enthusiasm Brod undertook to champion this young man and quickly established a relationship that in a strange way prefigured his role in Kafka's life. Yet unlike the unblemished twenty-two-year friendship that lasted until Kafka's death in 1924, this earlier relationship was doomed from the start.

The young man was Franz Werfel, whose world fame certainly does not rest on his poetry but on his later prowess as a biographer (*Verdi*), novelist (*The Song of Bernadette*), playwright (*Jakobowsky and the Colonel*), and third and last husband of Alma Mahler, relict of the composer Gustav Mahler and divorced wife of the architect Walter Gropius. Brod saw to it that Werfel's poems were published, first individually in the Sunday supplements of *Zeit,* a progressive Viennese daily that was soon to go under; and then in volumes of poems that Brod commended to his own (and Rilke's) publisher in Berlin, Axel Juncker. *Der Weltfreund* (Friend of the World), the first of these collections, contains a poem dedicated to Max Brod, who cites part of it in his autobiography, along with other acknowledgments that attest to Werfel's indebtedness. The verses themselves now seem curiously stilted and unconvincing, cast in a free form derived from Walt Whitman and from the French symbolist poet (and originator of *vers libre*) Jules Laforgue, whom both the young men revered. A fragment Brod particularly admired: "Woran erinnre ich mich heut? / An mein Kinderzimmer, wenn jemand an der Nähmaschine sass. / Vergessenes Duett: Nähmaschine und fistelndes Gas." (What picture floats down memory's lane? / My old nursery, while seams and broad hems through a sewing machine pass. / Forgotten old duet: sewing machine, the slow hiss of gas.) That is from the poem "Erster Frühling" (Early Spring), in which Werfel delicately traces the image that the as yet unplanted flower beds in a public park arouse in his mind's eye to the disorder of his erstwhile nursery.

Before long little disagreements began to crop up, even in fields in which they shared common tastes, above all music. Both admired Verdi, but Werfel's admiration centered on the early operas; he found the later masterpieces overblown, and he professed to abhor the music of Wagner—his fictionalized biography of Verdi starts with an imaginary near meeting between the two composers in the year before Wagner's death. Brod and Werfel both went to the opera whenever they could, even in their student days, when standing-room tickets were all they could afford. Brod records a delightful anecdote that Werfel told against himself in that connection. It seems that a prosperous family had invited him to join them in their box for a performance of *La forza del destino*. Werfel enjoyed the unaccustomed luxury of a loge seat thoroughly but proved to be something of a nuisance in that he sang along all his favorite arias, softly but with great expression and enthusiasm. At the end of the evening one of the party remarked that their next subscription performance would be *La Traviata*. "Oh, would you by any chance have a seat for me again?" asked Werfel. "Come by all means," was the answer, "you know we've never heard you in *Traviata*."

A disagreeable incident occurred when Brod was in Berlin to read from his own poems and happened to have with him the galleys of Werfel's *Weltfreund*, which Axel Juncker had just handed to him. On an impulse, Brod decided to introduce his protégé to Berlin and the world by treating the audience to a short preview of Werfel's verses. That reading elicited great enthusiasm and served to launch Werfel as a literary personality to be reckoned with. But one of the Berlin critics wrote that Brod had sought to prop up his own dull and shaky poetry by samples from the work of a greater master. Nothing could have been farther from the truth; but a Prague paper presently took up the same line, and a literary tempest in a teapot ensued that led Werfel to distance himself somewhat from his patron.

Worse was to come. As a result of the Jewish criticism of his novella *Ein tschechisches Dienstmädchen,* Brod had for the first time become aware of the awakening national spirit fostered by the Zionist movement organized by the Viennese journalist Theodor Herzl. Central Europe at the turn of the century was not a likely recruiting ground for immigration to Palestine (then a neglected backwater of the ailing Ottoman Empire); the movement was something of a joke to the wiseacres. "What is a Zionist?" went one canard. "It's a Jew who collects money from a second Jew to send a third Jew to Palestine." Yet Herzl was in dead earnest. In his book *Altneuland* (Old-New Land), a utopian novel in the manner of Edward Bellamy's *Looking Backward*, he produced a practical blueprint for a Western-style national state that was marred only by a boundless naiveté about the future role of the Arab population. But there was another aspect to Zionism. It was also an idealistic ideology that saw the in-gathering of the Jews in one place (not necessarily Palestine—other lands were suggested, for example Uganda) as merely the first step in the fulfillment of the tribe's manifest destiny, which was to pass on its spiritual and ethical values to all mankind and so to set it on its rightful path. This essentially optimistic phi-losophy had its detractors, Werfel among them, who took the view that mankind was doomed to unhappiness and misery be-cause it had sinned; its only hope lay in faith, not in worldly attempts at rescue and other good works.

That viewpoint inevitably led Werfel to Christianity. When he turned to Catholicism, his friendship with Brod was over, never to be fully repaired, although they were partially recon-ciled in old age. Brod considered Werfel's defection one of the greatest disappointments of his life and drew an analogy between Werfel and Boris Pasternak, a true proselytizing convert, whose strictures on Christianity sound such a strange note in *Dr. Zhivago*. More to the point, there is a much stronger echo of this *Gedankenkampf* in Brod's major novel, *Tycho Brahes Weg zu Gott* (which has appeared in English as *The Redemption of Tycho Brahe*), on which he was working while his conflict with Werfel was at its height. The famous Danish astronomer is shown in his relationship with the younger, more brilliant Johannes Kepler. (Both worked in Prague in the sixteenth century, under the patronage of the Hapsburg emperor Rudolf II.) Kepler is represented as the favorite of the gods, a genius to whom every-day concerns unrelated to his work are unimportant, including friendship and gratitude. Tycho Brahe is the older man, much more fate's pawn and less equipped to deal with a hostile world. (The contrast is heightened for artistic reasons: the historic per-sonalities were actually more alike, both victims of long neglect and unappreciated in their own times.) What struck Brod years later was the analogy inherent in the very letters of the protag-onists' names: Brahe–Brod, Kepler–Werfel—even in the first names: the y in Tycho is reminiscent of the x in Max (both letters are quite rare in German); and one variant of Kepler's Johannes

(Hans) is close to Werfel's Franz. Did Brod subconsciously choose the subject of his novel because of these analogies? It is possible.

Brod reserved his most scathing contempt for another convert, the Viennese publicist Karl Kraus, publisher of the pacifist and muckraking journal *Die Fackel* (Torch), which tended to turn the searing light of its satire equally on philistines and smug liberals. Kraus attacked not only the corrupt and the venal, but also the likes of Heine, Herzl, Werfel, Freud, and Hofmannsthal (all of whom happened to be of Jewish origin). Brod admired Kraus at first, although he had reservations about the sensationalism that sometimes seemed to land Kraus on the wrong side simply for the sake of réclame for his then still relatively unknown journal, as when he took against Dreyfus in the infamous affair in which a French officer of Jewish origin was wrongfully accused and condemned as a German spy. (It was this affair that had led Herzl to the prescient conclusion that the status of Jews in the diaspora would always remain parlous as long as they had no state of their own.) A truly shameful episode occurred during the war, a libelous attack in *Die Fackel* in which Brod was said to have fraudulently acquired the rights to the works of another enormously promising young poet, Franz Janowitz, who fell in the war while still in his twenties—a Bohemian Rupert Brooke. What had happened was that Brod, as always enthusiastic about new talent, had given a prominent place to the poor young man's sixteen poems in the literary yearbook *Arcadia,* which Brod edited. The facts were clear. Brod had exerted himself uncommonly on the young hopeful's behalf and had received a grateful acknowledgment from him. The poet's brother, the artist Hans Janowitz, was one of Kraus's intimates and admirers. (Hans Janowitz later achieved prominence as one of the creators of the famous German expressionist film *The Cabinet of Dr. Caligari*; he was a classmate of Werfel's, as was the famous actor Ernst Deutsch, who later became known to English-speaking audiences through his portrayal of the decadent aristocrat in Sir Carol Reed's film of Graham Greene's 1949 thriller *The Third Man.*) Kafka and Brod decided they would send copies of the correspondence with the dead poet to Hans Janowitz, in an effort to persuade Kraus to retract his unfounded accusations. Months went by, then Kafka received a laconic reply: Janowitz was in no position to forward the letters to Kraus; nor would Kraus be likely to pay attention to any explanation originating with Herr Brod. That episode was proof positive that Kraus was despicable, a view toward which Brod had tended ever since the beginning of the war, when the supposedly pacifist *Fackel* had at first suspended publication and then resumed with a thin issue containing Kraus's paean of praise for the noble, poetic words of the manifesto "To My Peoples," with which the aged Franz Josef I had called the nations of Austria-Hungary to arms.

It was during the war that Brod first came across Janáček. Brod was a talented pianist of near-professional caliber who enjoyed playing chamber music throughout his life—he once played a Mozart sonata with another well-known amateur, Albert Einstein, when the great physicist was a young professor in Prague—and studied composition with Adolf Schreiber, a student of Antonín Dvořák's, which made Brod describe himself facetiously as Dvořák's "grandson." He had also become a music critic and was a familiar figure in Prague's concert halls and opera houses. He was a great fan of Max Reger's and when that composer came to Prague to take part in some performances of his works, Brod was invited by the members of the Bohemian Quartet to join them in meeting Reger's train and help look after him—above all, to make sure he got him to the hall on time, since he was known to be a heavy drinker. The Bohemian Quartet was the first in the twentieth century's series of great chamber-music ensembles. It occupied a position comparable with that achieved later by such groups as the Rosé, Busch, Kolisch, and Budapest quartets, the Quartetto Italiano, and the Amadeus, Borodin, Guarneri, and Juilliard quartets. Brod especially liked the Bohemian Quartet's second violinist, Josef Suk—not the violin virtuoso of the present day but his grandfather of the same name, who was also Dvořák's composition student (and son-in-law) and is today perhaps the best-known Czech composer after Bedřich Smetana, Dvořák himself, Janáček, and Bohuslav Martinů. In the autumn of 1916 Brod suddenly received a note from Suk—the two had seen each other only once since the Reger recital three years before. Suk, who was that great rarity, an entirely selfless artist, wrote that Brod must on no account miss a performance of a new opera, *Její pastorkyňa* (Her Foster Daughter), by a newly discovered composer from Brno (Brünn), the provincial capital of Moravia. The performance was sold out. Brod had to revert to the habit of his student days and make do with a standing-room ticket above the second gallery, from where he could barely see the stage. But the acoustics were excellent, and the opening bars brought tears of bliss to his eyes. For the first time since the outbreak of war had so outraged his pacifist sensibilities, he could take heart again. If music like that was being heard in the midst of a murderous war, there must be some hope left for mankind. But who was the young composer, and how had he come to write such an opera (it was *Jenufa,* a title Brod himself gave it later) amid all the slaughter? To his surprise, the composer proved to be no youngster but a man of sixty-two; and to Brod's utter astonishment, he learned that the opera had been first performed in Brno in 1904 and had taken twelve years to reach even Prague. How could that have happened?

Janáček

In his sixties he was a handsome, stocky man with a full head of white hair, dark beetling eyebrows, and a white bristling mustache. There was a suggestion of great physical strength and stubborn persistence about him, the legacy of generations of skilled but unlettered weavers and simple country folk. Yet there was a gap in his family tree, as in the ancestry of many another great personage of humble origins (Abraham Lincoln, for one), that hinted at a quartering of more exalted lineage. His grandfather Jiří (George) was born four years after the great-grandfather's death. Six years later the widowed great-grandmother became the housekeeper of an unusually worldly and well-educated country priest, Antonín Herman, who had been an Augustinian functionary until his monastery was closed in one of Josef II's ecclesiastical reforms. It seems quite likely that Father Herman was also Jiří's father. At any rate, the little boy's prospects, which had been fairly dim, brightened considerably. He ultimately became a teacher and the father of seven children. One of them, another Jiří, followed his father into teaching, which in that place and at that time meant teaching music as well. Young Jiří got his first teacher's post when he was only sixteen. His evident musical talent soon attracted attention; he quickly rose to assistant teacher and choirmaster at Příbor, a small market town in the northeast corner of Moravia, halfway between Brno and Cracow. These provincial capitals were then both under Austrian rule, but the common folk spoke Czech in the one and Polish in the other. In Příbor they spoke Lachian, a dialect of Czech modulated by the softer Polish inflections. Promotion was slow. A decade later Jiří was thirty-three, married ten years and the father of five—and still only assistant teacher at Příbor. At that point, in the fateful year of 1848, he learned that a principal's post had fallen vacant in nearby Hukvaldy (Hochwald). This village of weavers and sheep farmers was so small (fewer than six hundred inhabitants) that its entire school consisted of one room, two blackboards, and two teachers—the principal and his assistant—who taught simultaneously. But it was a step up, and the ambitious Jiří took it eagerly. Over the next fifteen years he and his young wife Amalie (four years his junior and also a capable musician) had nine more children. The fifth was Leo Eugen, born in Hukvaldy on 3 July 1854, and known from the first by a local diminutive as Leoš.

Jiří's musical propensities were largely frustrated in Hukvaldy. Only the simplest masses could be performed in the tiny church. On feast days one might trek to the slightly larger neighboring parish of Rychaltice (Rychalt), whose church boasted a gilded organ, a pair of tympani, and a proper choir accompanied by whatever instrumentalists could be recruited from the countryside. One of Jiří's daughters, who played the viola, sometimes came along; and little Leoš, who could sing with perfect pitch from the age of seven, made a welcome addition to the soprano section. This talent led his father to seek to enroll the boy in the Queen's Monastery, an Augustinian school for choirboys in Brno, when he was only eleven. Many years before, as a novice teacher, the teenage Jiří had noticed a similarly talented boy among his pupils, a country girl's illegitimate son who was the victim of both poverty and prejudice. Jiří took an interest in the child, gave him free music and singing lessons, and helped him to a resident scholarship at a church school in Opava (Troppau). The boy, Pavel Křížkovský, did very well: he became an Augustinian and a fairly well-known composer of choral music, the founder of a distinctive Moravian choral style—and choirmaster at the Queen's Monastery. He would be Leoš Janáček's teacher, and out of gratitude to Jiří doubtless would look after the boy's body and soul as well. Who knows but Leoš might also decide to take holy orders—become an Augustinian monk like his preceptor (and like his putative great-grandfather)—or at least turn

Leoš Janáček. Drawing by Edvard Milén.

to the security of schoolteaching like his father and grandfather before him.

The Brno school had been endowed as a conservatory by a pious countess in 1648, the year of the Counter-Reformation's greatest triumph—the end of the Thirty Years' War. The original intent was to provide scholarships for promising sons of the poorer classes, some of whom might become monks or priests; in the rebellious Czech lands, bright and loyal candidates for the Church were hard to come by. A conservatory was originally not so much a place where "musickal vertues" and other arts might be conserved, but primarily an orphanage. The Bluebirds of the Queen's Monastery (so called after the boys' habits, light blue with white piping) literally had to sing for their supper daily, at the refectory table; and they were expected to perform at official receptions, at balls, masses, and funerals, even in concerts and operas. Each boy had to master the piano and at least one other instrument in addition to singing and music theory, all on top of a fairly heavy load of ordinary courses such as grammar, logic, and the humanities at the local German Realschule. Each place was greatly coveted; auditions and entrance examinations set a high standard. One of the monks was Gregor Mendel (1822–1884), the father of genetics, who conducted his then unknown pea hybridization experiments in the monastery garden; a fellow student was Alfons Mucha (1860–1939), later a successful art nouveau painter in Paris.

His first year under this demanding regimen was a difficult one for young Leoš. His father died in the middle of it, in his fiftieth year, a victim of the hard life at Hukvaldy. He left his widow with nine children, five of them under sixteen. The Queen's Monastery fed and housed its Bluebirds and supplied them with habits, but they had to pay for their textbooks and music lessons and buy shoes, everyday clothes, and other incidentals besides. A relatively affluent and childless uncle now came forward—his father's older brother Jan, a village priest—who undertook to provide for the boy's necessities; and when he ran short, Křížkovský quietly paid his school fees. No sooner had his situation returned to normal than a new disruption came along: war between Austria and Prussia. Leoš, too poor to go home during the summer vacation, stayed at the school; he was the only pupil left. All his schoolmates had gone home while the monastery had to help quarter the Emperor's troops, who were no match for Bismarck's Prussians. Within seven weeks, Austria had been thoroughly beaten, and her prestige had suffered a blow from which it never recovered. (One result was a strengthening of Czech national consciousness against Austrian absolutism.) A peace treaty was signed in August 1866. The new school year could start on time.

Leoš spent three more years at the school, until he was fifteen. He then went on to a three-year course at a state normal school for teachers, also in Brno, on a scholarship that required him to teach at a practice school without salary for two years after graduation. To make ends meet, he deputized for Křížkovský as choirmaster and organist, which earned him a place at the refectory table and occasional gifts of money. In his eighteenth year, a workmen's choral society elected him its choirmaster. He refused the emolument that went with the job, in part for idealistic reasons but also to keep his independence; the great thing was that he would gain a chance to perform his own first compositions. These early choral works were well received by the limited audiences that heard them but created no echo in the larger world. However, they served to clarify his own career plans. His official diploma entitled him to teach grammar, literature, geography, and history. But it now became quite clear to him that if he was to teach anything at all, it would have to be music. At the end of his two-year stint of practice teaching, he was appointed music teacher at his old teacher's college, but first he wangled a year's leave and enrolled at the organ school in Prague. Except for occasional gifts from well-wishers and a tiny stipend, he was completely without means.

Prague was a livelier environment for a budding musician. At one concert Leoš caught a glimpse of the aged Smetana. It was a benefit for that hero of Czech nationalism, who like Beethoven had become deaf toward the end of his life. It was also the world première of Smetana's *Vltava* (The Moldau), the symphonic poem destined to become the most popular of his cycle *Má vlast* (My Homeland). But concertgoing was a rare treat for the penniless Leoš. More often he was to be found in some church, picking up pointers from the resident organist—especially

St. Adalbert's, where that post was held by Antonín Dvořák. Besides, Leoš was intent on making the most of his year in Prague. To begin with, he was attempting to compress the three-year organist's course into a single year. On his own, he was studying esthetics, French, and Russian. And he was composing choral and organ pieces, in the austere manner fostered by the Cecilian movement, which viewed the increasingly elaborate sacred music of the day (epitomized by Beethoven's *Missa solemnis*) as too opulent for church performance and advocated a return to the simpler, predominantly *a cappella* style of the sixteenth century. (Both Křížkovský and Josef Foerster, the choirmaster at St. Adalbert's, were avid Cecilians.) All this frantic activity paid off. Leoš did complete the full course in the single academic year of 1874–75 and passed the examination that qualified him for an organist's post; and soon after that he also passed the state examination for music teachers. He resumed his Brno duties as music teacher at the state normal school and conductor of the workmen's choir. Before long, he switched to a more important choral society, the Brno *Beseda,* which drew its members from the better-heeled Czech bourgeoisie.

Although the *Beseda* was a more prosperous group, it had fallen upon hard times artistically. Under a new and energetic young conductor who was also a composer, its horizons expanded considerably. Janáček first turned it into a mixed choir, then added an orchestra, and was soon doing works such as Mozart's Requiem and Beethoven's *Missa solemnis*—not even the most fanatic Cecilian could object to its performance in the concert hall—and works by Křížkovský and by Dvořák, whom he had befriended during the year in Prague; one summer, they went on a walking tour together. Janáček also continued composing. For the first time he ventured beyond vocal music to suites for strings and chamber music, youthful pieces that show the influence of Liszt, Wagner, and Dvořák. By then the good burghers who ran the *Beseda* were growing restive about the excess of "serious" music that was being performed by what, after all, had started as a patriotic and social club that would hold an occasional musicale. The ambitious young conductor—he was still only twenty-five—was able to sidestep a confrontation by applying for another study leave, this time abroad. He had known for some time that he needed more formal training than he had received during his year in Prague. His departure would also postpone another, more personal crisis. He had fallen in love with one of his piano pupils, Zdenka (Sidonie) Schulz, the young daughter of the principal of the school where he taught. She was just fourteen, the only child of devoted parents who did not exactly relish this development. Janáček's leave was promptly granted. Principal Schulz even contrived to continue the young man's salary, by assuring the ministry in Vienna that no substitute would be needed—his colleagues would take up the slack among them—all in hopes that the engagement (which was not made public) would not survive the separation.

Where to go? Prague had the oldest conservatory, founded in 1811, but Janáček was seeking broader horizons. One of his goals was to improve his piano playing; perhaps he might make a living as a concert pianist. He had written to Anton Rubinstein, hoping to become his private pupil, but after following the great virtuoso all over Europe, the letter came back unopened. The only foreign language Janáček spoke with any assurance was German. Vienna, Berlin, Cologne all had well-known conservatories, as did many lesser towns, for example Frankfurt, where the sixty-year-old Clara Schumann was the principal piano teacher. In the end he opted for Leipzig, where the conservatory offered a broad choice of courses and where there were musicology lectures at the university besides. Almost greedily, he enrolled in every course he could, once more trying to cram a curriculum of three years into one. In addition to piano technique and playing, he signed up for harmony and counterpoint, musical form, organ, violin and chamber music, choral singing, and conducting; and he attended university lectures on the history of music.

Before long disenchantment set in. The instruction was far from progressive or even systematic; the facilities were derisory—the conservatory was then housed in a courtyard annex behind the Gewandhaus concert hall; the professors (except for Leo Grill, his composition teacher) seemed distinctly second-rate; and his fellow students spent untold hours aping the university fraternities by consuming prodigious quantities of beer. Instead of continuing in Leipzig, Janáček impulsively transferred to the Vienna Conservatory for the second semester, where composition was taught by Anton Bruckner and Franz Krenn; Janáček chose Krenn, who had also taught Gustav Mahler. (It was also much nearer to Brno and his beloved Zdenka.) But even Vienna proved unsatisfactory, especially after he was unfairly denied admission to a competition for student composers. Three months later the moody young man was back in Brno, pressing Zdenka, who was not quite fifteen, to marry him.

Apart from her age, other incompatibilities stood in the way, beginning with an ominous difference in temperaments. Her social standing was much higher, her upbringing absurdly genteel. She had been raised to speak German and not Czech (in which she was nonetheless fluent), except to the servants; whereas Janáček, although no blind chauvinist, was so uncompromisingly opposed to Austrian sovereignty that he would not even set foot in the German theater in Brno—a real deprivation, since there was as yet no Czech theater. Nevertheless, they were engaged on 1 July 1880. They were married a year later, two weeks before her sixteenth birthday. (Her parents' opposition may have been weakened by a *force majeure*—after sixteen years Zdenka's mother found herself pregnant again; Janáček was godfather to the new baby, who was called Leo.) The youthful bride was triumphantly borne off on a honeymoon that included visits to their relatives and to Dvořák and Křížkovský.

The next eight years were a time of furious activity that left the young husband little time for composition at first. At one point he held no fewer than nine posts in an unending struggle to make a living under conditions that would have driven a less determined champion of Moravian music to a more promising milieu. His home life was far from serene and not untouched by tragedy. He took out his frustration over his inability to compose on his hapless wife; their relationship deteriorated almost beyond repair. He longed for a son and was bitterly disappointed when their firstborn turned out to be a girl, who was given a Russian name, Olga, in keeping with Janáček's pan-Slavic leanings. Six months later the young couple separated. They reconciled after a somewhat peculiar second courtship, during which the fierce husband could be sometimes seen escorting his estranged wife to the theater, or at least to the portals—he still would not enter. They had a second child in 1888, the long-awaited son, who also received a Russian name, Vladimír; but he died of scarlet fever before he was three, and the parents became estranged once more, although they continued to live together.

Beginning in 1884 Janáček started composing again: some pieces for the organ, a few choral works based on folk themes, and then, during 1887, his first major work, the opera *Šárka*. The libretto was drawn from an epic by the minor Czech poet Julius Zeyer; the theme was based on an ancient legend of Czech Amazons whose cause comes to grief when their leader, Šárka, falls in love with the Siegfried-like hero, Ctirad. (The same legend is the theme of one of the six pieces in Smetana's *Má vlast*.) Six years before, Dvořák had encouraged Zeyer to make his poem into a play that might then serve as an opera libretto, but in the end had bowed out. Zeyer, who kept hoping that Dvořák would change his mind, would not cede the rights to Janáček, who in his inexperience had omitted to ask for them beforehand. That killed the opera's chances for good. It was not performed at all until 1925, after Janáček's repute was well established, and after another Czech composer, Zdeněk Fibich, had produced a successful opera on the same subject.

After this debacle Janáček began to turn away from romanticism. He had reached the age of thirty-five—the age at which Mozart died—without so much as establishing a personal style of composition; high time he developed one! At this point, fate intervened in the person of František Bartoš, the principal of a high school where Janáček taught singing, whose passion was collecting Moravian folk songs, even though he could barely notate them; usually he just wrote down the words. Janáček agreed to join him on his next field trip and was absolutely bowled over by the rich diversity of what he heard. He also found that Bartoš had been quietly bowdlerizing the rude rhymes of the honest country folk. For example, *Ani sem s ňú neřečňoval, / ani sem s ňú nestál* (of which a loose verse translation might be, Never did I wend my way there, / Never cared to wed her) on closer examination actually turned out to be, *Ani sem s ňú nenocoval, / ani sem s ňú nespal* (Never did I spend the night there, / Never dared to bed her). The two men spent several summers in what developed into a serious ethnographic collaboration, which culminated in a massive collection published by the Czech Academy at the turn of the century, containing over two thousand Moravian folk songs and a long musicological analysis by Janáček. Like the celebrated excursions into the countryside made by Béla Bartók, these trips had a profound effect on the composer's style. In a ballet commissioned by the National Theater in Prague, and in a one-act opera called *Počátek románu* (The Beginning of a Romance), Janáček made ample use of folk motives. His ballet enjoyed a modest success in Prague, his first work to make it to the Czech capital; the opera was performed only in Brno. These minor works are now overshadowed by his later oeuvre, which they prefigured in several respects, including the outside world's indifference to them and the fact that the one-acter was (like *Jenufa*) based on a work of Gabriela Preissová's. Even when Janáček expanded his ballet into a symphonic treatment, the *Lachian Dances* (in the manner of Smetana's *Bohemian Dances* and Dvořák's *Slavonic Dances*), no orchestra would play them for thirty years; and his Suite for Orchestra (1891) suffered the same fate. All the same, these works, and a spate of shorter compositions, mark the beginning of an individual, characteristic style in the music of Janáček, who is sometimes put down as "the Czech Musorgsky." There are parallels between the two composers, but they are not the result of emulation. Although Musorgsky was fifteen years older and was well established in Russia before Janáček was out of his teens, his works were then seldom performed in Central Europe, and Janáček never heard a note of *Boris Godunov* (1874) until long after he had written *Jenufa,* not even during a long-planned visit to Russia in 1896.

He had yearned to go there ever since his student days, when he had wanted to take piano lessons from Anton Rubinstein; now his brother František in St. Petersburg sent him a ticket. The distaste for all things Austrian made him such a Russophile that he was quite ready to overlook tsarist oppression even in Slav lands such as Poland and the Ukraine, not to speak of the forced russification of the hinterlands. On reaching his goal, the Exhibition of Industry and Art in Nizhni Novgorod, he exclaimed over a model exhibit intended for Central Asia: "Look at that! How proud and happy I am at the thought that a Slav nation can spread enlightenment, too." But he heard no music during the two-week trip (it was July) except a memorial concert for Rubinstein. Nevertheless, the Russian Orthodox vocal tradition emanating from even the humblest church exerted a lifelong influence on Janáček's music and was to be reflected in some of his most important works, most directly in the *Glagolitic Mass*. A more immediate result of his preoccupation with Slavonic themes in both sacred music and folklore was a strengthening of the resolve to get on with the work that was to become his magnum opus and one of the landmarks of the twentieth-century operatic repertory, *Jenufa*.

Janáček himself did not remember afterward exactly when the first creative impulse formed in his mind, but from external evidence it must have been in 1894. It was to be a long travail: the work was not finished until the beginning of 1903, when Janáček was forty-eight. Gabriela Preissová's play *Her Foster Daughter* had its première in Prague in 1890 and was produced two years later in Brno, where a Czech theater had been founded at last. The play (later expanded into a novel) is a story of passion, wrongdoing, and retribution drawn from peasant life, a genre whose best-known exemplar is Pietro Mascagni's 1890 opera *Cavalleria rusticana,* based on a short story and play by Giovanni Verga that had been a famous vehicle for Eleanora Duse. Jenufa (Genevieve) is seduced by her boastful rich cousin Števa (Stephen) and secretly bears his child, but he refuses to marry her and becomes engaged to the village mayor's daughter; his stepbrother Laca (Ladislaus), who has always loved Jenufa, then offers to marry her but having heard rumors about a baby questions her stepmother about it. The stepmother, a somber and revered figure who is the vestry keeper of the village *kostel* (church) and is thus known as Kostelnička, is so bent on salving the family's honor that she tells him a lie—that the little boy has died—and is then panicked into making it come true by drowning the child. The dénouement comes on the morning of Jenufa's wedding to Laca: the baby has been found under the melting ice, Jenufa and Števa are identified as the parents (whereupon his bride renounces him), and Kostelnička publicly confesses her guilt and is arrested. Unlike the typical *verismo* melodrama, the piece ends on a note of promised happiness and serenity: Laca, steadfast in his love and full of admiration for Jenufa's courage, offers to marry her despite all and is accepted.

Reams have been written about the musical sources of *Jenufa*, which include not only folklore and Old Church Slavonic (which is to say ultimately Greek) modes, but also a feature that has come to be almost uniquely identified with Janáček: the highly original use of so-called speech melodies, musical reproductions of the natural inflections of the Czech tongue, particularly of the lilting country dialect of Moravia. (While working on *Jenufa* he had begun the practice he continued for the rest of his life of noting them down systematically wherever he could, like a musicologist double of Bernard Shaw's Professor Higgins.) But *Jenufa* is much more than a folk opera or a Moravian counterpart of Bohemia's *Bartered Bride,* and Janáček is no mere "Smetana in a minor key," as Max Brod was to describe him. (That phrase must have appalled Janáček, who did not think too highly of Smetana.) The work is suffused with innovative harmonies, brilliant orchestration, telling psychological effects, and a sure dramatic line that never slackens. The speech melodies are especially important because Gabriela Preissová's words are frequently used almost verbatim. Other composers were beginning to write operas to prose librettos, notably Debussy, but *Pelléas et Mélisande* (1902) was set to the prose of a great poet, Maurice Maeterlinck, not verismo folk drama; whereas Janáček skillfully exploited the speech melodies and their artful repetition to create a no less poetic effect from much humbler materials. Although folk themes sometimes appear in the work in unalloyed form, especially in dances and peasant songs, the use Janáček generally makes of them is rarely direct or primitive; rather, they are transformed through his genius into an expression of the highest art. In Jenufa's heartrending dirge for her dead child, Janáček drew on his own painful memories of little Vladimír's death. Nor had he yet drained the bitter cup to the dregs. His daughter Olga, grown into a beautiful and slender girl of nineteen who was preparing to become a teacher of Russian, suffered from heart disease, the legacy of a childhood infection. To guard her from the consequences of an unhappy love affair, her parents seized an opportunity to send her for a prolonged stay in Russia, where she was further weakened by an attack of typhoid fever. She died in Brno the following winter, in her twentieth year. During her last illness she pathetically begged her father to play from *Jenufa* for her, since she would never hear it performed—she had already received extreme unction. Janáček consecrated the work to Olga's memory; the dedication is in Russian. Almost overnight, his hair turned gray.

As soon as *Jenufa* was finished, it went off to Prague, since the Czech theater in Brno lacked the resources for a full production. The chief of the National Theater's opera wing was the composer-conductor Karel Kovařovic, whom Janáček had unfortunately antagonized sixteen years before by a harsh review of an opera Kovařovic had written and had managed to get performed in his early twenties. A month went by. Would the now all-powerful music director overlook this youthful contretemps? With some trepidation, Janáček inquired when he might expect a decision. Kovařovic did not reply; the brusque letter rejecting the opera was signed by the theater's manager, Gustav Schmoranz. *Jenufa* would have to be produced in Brno after all.

SCHMORANZ TO JANÁČEK, 28 APRIL 1903

> I sincerely regret we cannot accept your opera for production. We should like to see a staging of your work meet with a complete success for you as well as for us, but fear that your work would not achieve such a success.
>
> We return the score and piano score to you herewith.

Janáček was shaken. Instead of the elation an artist might expect to feel on perfecting what would turn out to be the greatest achievement of his life, he found himself at a particularly low ebb. He had lost his beloved daughter; his marriage had gone sour; he was up to his neck in the daily drudgery of instructing indifferent students at the normal school for teachers, and even the more committed students at his own organ school (which was actually a small conservatory) were often exasperating; none of the other compositions he had written while he worked on *Jenufa* had been published or performed outside Moravia, except for transcriptions of some of the folk songs and dances he had collected with Bartoš; and now this fresh blow to his fragile self-confidence, the rejection of his masterpiece by the leader of his country's prime operatic showcase.

Still, life went on. The Brno première of *Jenufa* came and went; the work was enthusiastically reviewed, remained in the repertory for three consecutive seasons, and was revived in 1911 and 1913. (In its second season, Kovařovic came to hear it at last, but that did not change his mind.) Most important, Janáček continued composing and pursuing his theoretical studies, not only in music but in philology, esthetics, even sociology. Among the works that stem from this period is his *Complete Textbook of Harmony*, in which he advanced the highly idiosyncratic theory that chords are best resolved by means of tones that are "virtual"—that is, evoked only in the imagination or the "inner ear" by reverberations of "actual" tones (and their harmonics) sounded previously. (This theory has not found many adherents and was not rigorously followed even in Janáček's own compositions, but it had the salutary effect of freeing him from the harmonic constraints that had dominated nineteenth-century music since the days of Beethoven.)

This was also the period during which he wrote several chamber works that have since gained a place in the international repertory, notably the piano cycles *On an Overgrown Path* and *In the Mists,* the *Fairytale* for cello and piano (written in 1910, the same year as Igor Stravinsky's *Firebird,* and like it based on a Russian legend), the Violin Sonata, several choral works (including some on socially conscious themes, such as *Maryčka Magdónova*), and the greater part of a comic opera, *Mister Brouček's Excursions.* This last, based on two satires that the popular novelist Svatopluk Čech had published in 1888 and 1889, at the same time and in the same genre as Mark Twain's *A Connecticut Yankee in King Arthur's Court,* is about a Prague burgher's dreams in which he is twice transported totally out of his element, first to the moon and then to the Hussite warriors of the fifteenth century. The creation of this work was a real-life farce. So many writers had taken a hand in the libretto that the composer was afterward led to express himself about it along the lines of "Hail, hail, the gang's all here!" The endeavors of one of them, Viktor Dyk, were broken off when he was arrested in 1916 and convicted of fomenting civil disobedience by a newspaper serial in which the ineptitudes of Austria-Hungary's wartime authorities were mercilessly ridiculed under the guise of an adventure story that described parallel conditions in tsarist Russia. Long before that Janáček's interest in the work (which was not completed until the end of 1917) had begun to waver, for an opportunity had meanwhile arisen to have *Jenufa* produced in Prague at last.

The Friends of Art Club in Brno, which Janáček had helped to found in the nineties, had published the piano score of *Jenufa* in 1908. Through the club's president, the physician František Veselý, Janáček came to know a remarkable woman, the singer and writer Marie Calma, who at her father's request had forsaken an operatic career for the concert stage and the propagation of folk music. He met her in Veselý's home just after an unbound copy of the piano score had arrived from the printer, the pages still uncut. Janáček cut a few pages, sat down at the piano, and said to her: "They say you're a fine singer—let's see what you can do!" To his astonishment, she faultlessly sight-read portions of Jenufa's and Kostelnička's parts. They became fast friends and saw each other often, especially after she became the widowed Veselý's wife and moved to Brno. It was probably at her suggestion that the Friends of Art Club resolved (Janáček dissenting) that Dr. Veselý should take the bull by the horns, bypass Kovařovic, and appeal privately and directly to the chairman of the National Theater's board of governors, Dr. Jaroslav Hlava, who was a distinguished pathologist and thus a professional colleague. In his answer, Hlava pointed out—as governors of opera companies have been known to do before and since—that the problem was above all financial: his undersubsidized house had responsibilities toward a whole slew of deserving Czech composers.

HLAVA TO VESELÝ, 25 FEBRUARY 1911

I cannot give you a satisfactory reply to your *private* (?) letter in regard to Janáček's opera.

Mr. Kovařovic did not accept this opera at the time for various reasons, among which the financial standpoint certainly played a part. For preparing an opera costs at least 4–6 weeks of intensive work and if it then finds no favor with a wider public, the theater takes an irretrievable loss. Kovařovic is on the whole quite receptive toward the younger generation, but from a practical standpoint we can concede him only one or two experiments a year.

Now it is the turn of Novák's *Storm* [actually, not an opera but a symphonic work], Picka's *Rainer the Painter* [it died after five performances], and further Foerster's newly revised *Jessica.*

We have given Zich's *The Painter's Idea* and Piskáček's opera *Wild Barbara* [three performances apiece], and Ostrčil's *Blossom* [six performances]. Besides that, we are also being importuned to cultivate Fibich. What first, then?

Our government subvention amounts to 128,000 crowns; our annual budget is 1.5 million. On top of that, the City of Prague's beggarly 15,000 crowns has been reduced to 10,000. Where shall we find the money? Try and find a Maecenas in Moravia like the Germans have for the staging of Wagner's operas and then we might do something.

Mr. Janáček has revised his original opera [some minor changes had been made for the 1911 revival in Brno] and would be willing to make further revisions—I think that proves it is not the *chef d'œuvre* you imagine. Mr. Janáček would do better to write something new, then I shall see what I can do for him in the foreseeable future.

I have expressed myself quite frankly—to be sure, not for publication—my letter is only a gloss on the answer the management will send you if you will let me know whether the letter you sent me was an official one.

The crack about productions of Wagner's operas was evidently occasioned by the more generous subsidies the German opera house in Prague was getting. The composer had stipulated that *Parsifal* should never be staged outside Bayreuth, where a theater had been built and dedicated exclusively to a short annual season of his works. He soon relented, to the point of discussing the inclusion of *Parsifal* in the repertory of a touring company organized for the production of Wagner operas by the impressario Angelo Neumann, but died before any arrangements were completed. His widow Cosima Wagner resolutely kept the work in Bayreuth for another twenty years; when the Metropolitan's manager Heinrich Conried undertook to stage it in 1903, she tried to block the production but found that the protection of the German law did not extend to New York. After the American première (and the twelve sold-out performances that followed it), European opera houses would not be denied. Neumann, who meanwhile had been appointed manager of the German opera in Prague, became something of a specialist in productions of Wagner operas, which did not come cheap.

Angelo Neumann's rule in Prague (1885–1910) inaugurated a golden age for the German opera there that lasted over fifty years. (Competition with the Czech opera led to some absurd situations: when a performance of *Parsifal* was sanctioned at last, both houses scheduled the première on the same day; ultimately, they agreed tacitly to give the Czechs first dibs on new French works and the Germans on German ones.) The first conductor Neumann engaged was Gustav Mahler, who was in charge during 1885–86. Among his successors were Arthur Bodanzky (1907–1909) and Otto Klemperer (1907–1910); Alexander von Zemlinsky (1911–1927); William Steinberg (1927–1929); and George Szell (1929–1937), and, in association with Szell, Max Rudolf, Fritz Zweig, and Walter Susskind—all of whom later went on to successful careers in Britain and America. So did Mahler, who conducted in New York repeatedly during the last five years of his life but never settled in America; he had gone from Prague to Vienna, and from 1900 until his death in 1911 he directed the opera house there.

It would never have occurred to a man of Janáček's convictions to offer his work to Angelo Neumann at the German opera house in Prague, but he saw no objection to submitting it to the Imperial and Royal Opera House in Vienna. After all, he reasoned, the "Royal" referred to the monarch's title as King of Bohemia—he was also the Margrave of Moravia—so the Vienna house belonged to Czechs, too. (For a parallel situation, one would have to imagine a Quebec playwright who might hate to have a first Montreal performance of his piece staged in English, but would be thrilled to get an English production in London.) An invitation to come to Brno to hear *Jenufa* had gone to Gustav Mahler in Vienna as early as 1904. Unlike Kovařovic, Mahler was no opera composer manqué (except for two abortive attempts in his youth, he never wrote an opera himself) and held no grudge against Janáček; in fact, he had probably never heard of him. But Mahler's reply uncovered a new obstacle.

MAHLER TO JANÁČEK, 9 DECEMBER 1904

. . . It is unfortunately not possible for me to get away from here in the near future. However, since I am certainly interested in becoming acquainted with your work, I beg you to send me the vocal score with a German text at your convenience.

The situation was not without its ironies. Mahler had specified a German version; could he not have made out the Czech text? Like Janáček, Mahler was born in a Moravian village. He grew up in the nearby garrison town of Jihlava (Iglau); the brass bands and folk themes of his childhood weave in and out of his compositions. Before his triumphs in Prague and Vienna he had conducted at the opera house in Olomouc (Olmütz) in northern Moravia. Yet the Jewish provincial family into which he was born aspired to be genteel (and, ultimately, Gentile: to get the Vienna job, Mahler had become a Catholic). Little Gustav had been brought up to speak only German, not Czech—much as a Jewish boy in Cardiff would be expected to speak English, not Welsh. He had doubtless picked up Czech from other children in Jihlava and during his stays in Olomouc and Prague. The Czech composer J. B. Foerster recalls in his autobiography, *The Pilgrim* (1947), that when he and Mahler both worked in Hamburg in the 1890s Mahler corrected an unsatisfactory German libretto of Smetana's *Bartered Bride,* "since he understood the Czech text." Yet in 1904 he refused to evaluate the dramatic aspects of *Jenufa* from the Czech libretto and asked for a German translation. None existed at the time; and that was that.

It is difficult for us to realize that the musical life of Central Europe continued throughout the war years of 1914–1918—that concerts, recitals, and opera productions went on virtually unimpeded. (That was certainly not what happened in Europe during the Second World War, with its air raids and massive dislocations of whole populations.) Although the First World War was much more costly in military casualties, the civilian population remained relatively unscathed, at least in the hinterlands; and it was precisely then that *Jenufa* got its chance in Prague and Vienna. Effort and chance both played a part. The effort came through the unrelenting endeavors of Marie Calma; the chance, because she happened to find a new avenue to the implacable Kovařovic, who had been her singing teacher and was now the chief of opera at Prague's National Theater.

Marie Calma's husband, František Veselý, had been called up with the reserves at the beginning of the war as the medical officer of his regiment, even though he was in his fifties, but had had to resign his commission and his post as chief of the military hospital at Kroměříž (Kremsier) after a political incident: he had refused to rise for a toast to the Emperor's noble ally, the German Kaiser. (This episode would stand him in good stead after the war: he became one of the Czechoslovak republic's top health officials.) He was immediately appointed medical director of an up-and-coming spa in northeastern Bohemia, Bohdaneč. The appointment turned out to be an important milestone in Marie Calma's campaign for *Jenufa*. The man who was to prove crucial to it liked to spend his vacations at Bohdaneč because he had been born there. This was Karel Šípek (a pen name meaning "brier"; his real name was more pedestrian, Josef Peška), a well-known writer, music critic, translator—among other things he had translated Brandon Thomas's 1892 farce *Charley's Aunt* into Czech—and, more to the point, Kovařovic's librettist. Marie Calma made his acquaintance in Bohdaneč and immediately invited him to a soirée at which she sang several of Jenufa's arias. Šípek was captivated at once and insisted that she must sing them also for his good friend Gustav Schmoranz, the manager of the National Theater, who was coming to spend a day with him in Bohdaneč. When he arrived, the energetic Marie Calma was in the middle of another project—she was mounting an exhibition of the work of Czech painters in the spa's colonnade, to help them through the difficult war years—but she broke off this work without a qualm to give Schmoranz an audition in her apartment. He was likewise most enthusiastic and promised to do what he could with Kovařovic. If it came to a production, he asked, would Mme. Calma like to sing the title role? Would she! Sensing victory, she sent the piano score off to Prague once more.

The sequence of these events, subsequently confirmed by Marie Calma, gave rise to a more fanciful—not to say operatic—account that was still making the rounds in 1969, when the second edition of Max Brod's autobiography came out. According to this version, she had concocted the following plot with Šípek. She would sing excerpts from the opera on three successive days, with her windows open, while he would entice Schmoranz to pass by at the appropriate hour. Schmoranz came, heard, and was conquered; and the path to an early production had been smoothed.

Unfortunately, what happened next belies this story. At Schmoranz's insistence, Kovařovic "restudied" the piano score, but his decision was once more negative. The arguments marshaled against the opera show how difficult it was for Janáček's unique style to make its way against the musical establishment even in his own country. Kovařovic liked the prayer in the first act and some of the soliloquies, Schmoranz reported to Šípek—anything that relied on the form of the Slovak song—but had serious reservations about all the rest. It simply failed to meet the minimum requirement for the acceptance of new works that he had announced when he became chief of opera—that they be free of technical flaws.

SCHMORANZ TO ŠÍPEK, 29 SEPTEMBER 1915

. . . Yet [according to Kovařovic] the dialog is totally faulty. On the one hand the composer consistently follows the principle of the tonal effect of the spoken Moravian-Slovak tongue; on the other, altogether contrary to all rules of actual speech, he makes the singers repeat certain places in the text x times.

Where then is there any stylistic principle? [Kovařovic] says it is a curious mix of entirely new "novelty" with regional primitivism (bordering on impotence in composition) and an old-fashioned manner long since overtaken. His restudy of the work had reaffirmed Kovařovic's original view of the matter. And he is glad that his former judgment had in no way wronged the matter.

You cannot doubt that he would be glad to do you a favor. But he cannot advance the matter against his artistic conviction.

This letter drove Šípek to a white fury. Kovařovic was a person to be reckoned with. The National Theater had provided Šípek with commissions in the past and might be expected to do so again in the future. Yet he now threw all caution to the winds and lit into Schmoranz in a reply that not only blasted his theater and Kovařovic for their limited outlook and poor judgment, it also contained a prescient estimate of Janáček's true worth.

ŠÍPEK TO SCHMORANZ, OCTOBER 1915

. . . He was wrong then and he is wrong now, our dear maestro [Kovařovic].

I remember what he had to say about *Rusalka* [he had underestimated the subsequent popularity of Dvořák's opera] when he was studying it. . . . That's why he has an uneven repertory, a patchy ensemble.

You will give *Walküre* without having a Walküre, just as you gave *Libuše* [Smetana's opera] without a Libuše. You are just like the Catholic church. You'll mumble over the wafer, over the wine, you'll declare: this is the body, this is the blood, and you expect people to believe it.

You let *Butterfly* flutter by [it had been relinquished to Prague's City Theater at Vinohrady], yet you landed a dead fish in *Julien* [Charpentier's opera died after six performances]. You paved the way for *Quality Street* at Smíchov [Sir James Barrie's play was a success at another suburban theater]; meanwhile, you netted *The Admirable Crichton* [another Barrie piece; six performances], with Mušek as the solo carp. You transfused *Polish Blood* [Oskar Nedbal's popular 1913 operetta] to Vinohrady and your box office suffers from anemia. . . . What is most rotten in your state of Denmark is the dramaturgy, both operatic and dramatic. Both *unter Luder* [a slightly misquoted piece of German slang meaning "abominable"]. If it is true that one learns from one's mistakes, you must be learning all the time.

I come back to where I started: If the Maestro had gone to hear [Janáček's] *Maryčka Magdónova* as sung by the Moravian Teachers' Choir [in Prague; they had previously sung it in Paris], he would not have put down Janáček for a rank beginner. He would not have permitted himself the tactlessness of scheduling the young prophet Jeremaiah's opera [another failure: a one-acter, based on Rémy de Gourmont's *The Old King,* by the twenty-six-year-old Jaroslav Jeremiáš], over whose libretto you threw up your hands, while turning down a man of sixty who had composed a genuine Moravian folk drama. But of course: infallibility above all other considerations.

Two things weighed with the Maestro: personal and fundamental distaste, and substantive incomprehension.

I have no objection to your showing this letter to Kovařovic.

It is not clear whether Kovařovic was in fact shown the letter. Schmoranz might have thought it the better part of valor to withhold it, especially since he knew that the fifty-year-old Šípek had another reason for being in a foul temper: he had lost the use of his right hand after a stroke and was teaching himself to manage with his left, a particular frustration for a writer. The prickly Šípek was quite prepared to break with Kovařovic over *Jenufa*. The summer season at Bohdaneč was over. Marie Calma had returned to Prague with her husband for the winter, and Šípek was about to follow suit. He would make one last attempt.

Šípek to Marie Calma, 31 October 1915

. . . When I get back I shall ask Kovařovic to come and see me and we shall have a talk about *Jenufa*. Maybe that will put paid to our friendship for life, but I feel it incumbent upon me to open my trap once more. . . .

Kovařovic saw Šípek on November 10 and Marie Calma a week later. He doubtless got an earful from Schmoranz, too. The incessant pleas, by people whose judgment Kovařovic trusted, began to make an impression at last. His resolve softened. Perhaps the production he had heard in Brno in 1904 had not done the work full justice. He would have to see what he could do to save face if retreat was not to turn into a rout. Could he have another look at the piano score? And would Marie Calma sing for him any soprano aria he designated? Most important, would Janáček object if a few changes were made?

The last request would require a tactful approach to the fiercely independent composer, but since so much hinged on it, maybe he could be persuaded. Marie Calma's husband undertook to act as the middleman.

. . . [Kovařovic] is in principle no longer opposed to the production—for the present he puts the blame on the wartime—on
the contrary he is evidently prepared to perform *Jenufa*, only
later. I think that he will soften even further once he hears my
wife's interpretation and that he will—as we would wish—direct
Jenufa in the spring of 1916 *himself*. He does not want his retreat
to be an abrupt one.

He mentioned that he found some passages very beautiful,
especially the last scene—it is fine music even without the voices.
And he said, "Actually, why shouldn't I perform Janáček, even
if I don't fancy this or that passage, when I perform modern
stuff that I do not fancy at all?!"

Send the score by return mail so that the matter is not held
up. He would be pleased if you would—but it may not come to
that—express your willingness to change a few things. It seems
they would be *trivial*; it would be rather an expression of good
will.

It is known that K. made changes even in Smetana.

The overall impression of the conversation was very favorable; Peška [i.e., Šípek] must have worked him over thoroughly.

All seemed to depend now on Marie Calma, whose audition
was set for December 8. Janáček wired encouragement: "May
you break through!" The audition was a success, but Kovařovic
wanted to deal with Janáček from a position of strength and get
him to agree to revisions in principle *before* the commitment to
a production had been made. Both Marie Calma and her husband now wrote Janáček, practically begging him to agree. What
Veselý did not say was that Kovařovic had volunteered a curious
bit of information: if Janáček were no longer living and thus not
on hand to object to revisions, the opera would have been produced long since; the truth, pure and simple, was that Kovařovic
had continued to reject the work because he was genuinely convinced that the score wanted improvement. But the truth, as
Oscar Wilde remarked, is rarely pure, and never simple.

To the astonishment of all parties, Janáček went out of his
way to be affable. Age had not mellowed him, quite the contrary,
but for once he would desist from practicing what Brod later
called, in reference to Janáček (and quoting the phrase in the

original English), *the fine art of making enemies*. He sent off the score at once, with a most conciliatory letter.

JANÁČEK TO KOVAŘOVIC, 10 DECEMBER 1915

Mme. Calma Veselá has sent me a note that certainly made me glad. Why wouldn't I accept your suggestions for possible cuts! You may be sure I shall accept them with thanks.

Whatever you think appropriate shall be done. On the contrary, I beg you to be kind enough to make the revisions.

Mme. Calma-Veselá gives me hope that you might rehearse and conduct the work yourself—then I really would be at a loss to know how to repay my debt to you.

I look forward to receiving your suggestions.

One obstacle still remained: the financial risk of a new production so late in the season, when the theater's budgetary reserves would be low. Veselý resolved it most generously by a personal guarantee: if the projected six performances were not sold out, he said, he would make up the difference out of his own pocket.

With this last obstacle overcome, planning for the production could go forward, including casting. The first performance was scheduled for the following spring. Janáček came to Prague at Christmas to carry out the revisions suggested by Kovařovic. The two men had not met for years. (Once, when Kovařovic was told during the dress rehearsal of another opera that Janáček had slipped into the house, he had had him thrown out.) Was Kovařovic hoping to mount a revised production without a direct encounter? Marie Calma and her husband again acted as go-betweens. Janáček had expressed the hope that he could join them in their box for a holiday performance of Smetana's *Libuše*; Kovařovic was conducting. During the intermission Veselý took Janáček backstage to see Kovařovic; a sticky moment. The two men shook hands—then embraced; old-time grudges were forgotten. Janáček returned to the box in high good humor. "All fixed!" he beamed at Marie Calma. He had already forgotten how much effort had gone into bringing matters even to this pass.

Worse was to come. Marie Calma assumed she would be

given the title role. Kovařovic had been her first opera teacher, when she was fifteen; she thought he wanted her to have the part. Still, the decision was not his alone. It would smack of favoritism to assign the title role in what promised to be an important première to a singer who was not a member of the theater's regular company and who had not been anywhere near an opera stage in years. On the other hand, ever since Schmoranz had first heard her sing the *Jenufa* excerpts, it seemed to be understood that the part would go to Marie Calma. Yet she did not want to put herself in the position of applying for it. The most she would do was to ask Janáček to inquire whether she should be preparing the part.

Janáček hesitated. Should he risk wearing out his hard-won welcome with Kovařovic? Perhaps the management could be quietly persuaded of the justice of Marie Calma's claim to a part in the production. Yes, that was it: after all, who had done more to bring it about? Janáček told her to go ahead and learn Jenufa's part, it was "all fixed." Only it wasn't: a few weeks later he had to write her sheepishly that it was all off—the part would go to Kamila Ungrová, a member of the regular ensemble. Bitterly disappointed, Marie Calma blamed Janáček for this outcome.

MARIE CALMA TO JANÁČEK, 25 FEBRUARY 1916

. . . For it was my Jenufa that persuaded Kovařovic and overcame his objections of a hundred different sorts that it was unsingable and so on—and my profound conviction of the beauty of your work helped to defend it and to gain its victory.

Now that the first purpose of all—to get your *Jenufa* to the National—has been achieved, now that I have stopped regretting the hard work that went into preparing a role that has become part of my life's blood and soul, I cannot but tell you of my disappointment, which comes down to just one thing—that you did not or could not find it in your heart to say, "I want Mme. Calma to sing Jenufa because I feel that no one else would sing it so well. . . ."

Janáček made excuses, but they did not ring true. Three weeks later, when the Moravian conductor Jožka Charvát asked him to recommend his wife for the role, Janáček wrote Kovařovic, "It goes without saying that it wouldn't occur to me to interfere with your casting." The friendship with Marie Calma and her husband cooled off considerably. Janáček sought to make amends. The Veselýs had meanwhile returned to Bohdaneč for the spa's new season. Janáček commissioned his old Brno friend František Mareš, who was Veselý's cousin, to stop off at Bohdaneč on his way to the Prague première on 26 May 1916 and convey his personal invitation to them. Mareš was unable to make the detour but sent a long telegram begging them to come and to renew the friendship. The telegram reached them a day before the première. They wired back their best wishes—and regrets.

The rage over the lost role was not the only reason the friendship had ended. During the rehearsals for *Jenufa* Janáček had met the glamorous Gabriela Horvátová, who took the part of Kostelnička in the production. (She had been the protégé of the composer-conductor Otakar Ostrčil, who ultimately succeeded Kovařovic at the National Theater; she was to have a hand in that appointment, by persuading Kovařovic's first choice, Fric Sommer, to withdraw.) Her boundless enthusiasm for the opera infected the entire cast; much of the work's success in Prague— and hence in the world—must be credited to her. Janáček was greatly drawn to her. Both were married; he was sixty-one, she was thirty-eight. Their friendship developed into a passionate, no-holds-barred affair. For the next two years they could scarcely bear to be apart for a moment. He consulted her on everything, from his dealings with the authorities to matters of great artistic import. Their surviving letters border on the torrid. Their friends were scandalized. Marie Calma's heart went out to Janáček's wife, who had confided in her during a visit to Bohdaneč (and that summer was driven to attempt suicide).

In a "background letter" to a volume of Janáček's correspondence with her and her husband, Marie Calma wrote:

> The confidences that Mrs. Janáček poured forth immediately upon her arrival in Bohdaneč made me realize the full depth of her misery. The period that signified advancement and worldly success for Janáček was full of humiliating experiences for her. Janáček's boundless recklessness played itself out in an untam-

able storm. If Janáček is now and again portrayed as a person of sense and sensibility, that is either a deliberate attempt not to show him in his true colors or failure to understand the texture of so complex a personality. One could write an interesting, fascinating novel about him. But would that advance his cause? His artistic contribution is so great that it outweighs the human flaws in his character.

(Four years later Marie Calma did sing Jenufa at the National Theater after all. Her performance—one of the last arranged by Kovařovic, who died seven months later—took place on 6 May 1920. Janáček wrote her an impersonal note wishing her success and reiterating that it had not been within his power to have the part assigned to her at the 1916 première. They met only once after that, at the festival of the International Society for Contemporary Music held in Prague in 1925. She died in Prague in 1966, aged eighty-five. Gabriela Horvátová outlived her: she died, also in Prague, in 1968, aged ninety-one.)

The Prague production of *Jenufa* marked a distinct turn in Janáček's fortunes. During the twelve years between the Brno and Prague premières he had been too discouraged to compose much. The success in Prague and all that followed on it gave him fresh incentive. So did the end of the war and of three centuries of the hated Hapsburg rule, and the elation over his country's independence, which gave promise of a better chance for the reception of Czechoslovak music abroad. During the twelve years that remained to him he wrote some of his finest music, including (in addition to *Taras Bulba*) another four operas. And it all began with the extraordinary success of the eight sold-out performances of *Jenufa* in the spring of 1916 and of the eighteen repeat performances during the 1916–17 season. Richard Strauss, who came to Prague that autumn to conduct a Sunday-afternoon performance of no fewer than three of his tone poems by the Czech Philharmonic, heard *Jenufa* the same evening, on 15 October 1916, and gave his qualified approval. (He liked the dramatic tension of the last act—as well he might—but thought the piece was technically "somewhat mannered.") Three weeks later the listener whose opinion was to prove most decisive for Janáček's future heard the opera for the first time: Max Brod.

First Collaboration

Brod's first enthusiasm was expressed in an essay he wrote soon after he saw *Jenufa*, five months after the Prague première, for the Berlin theatrical weekly *Schaubühne*. The review, entitled "Tschechisches Opernglück" (The Good Fortune of Czech Opera), appeared on 15 November 1916; it was reprinted in Czech translation in Prague and Brno. Janáček sent Brod a note of appreciation and received an admiring reply and an invitation. Janáček turned up a few days later. He had suddenly got it into his head (he said) that Brod was just the man to introduce his work to the world. Fitting action to the thought, he rushed down to the Brno station and jumped on the next train to Prague, where he arrived at six o'clock on a Sunday morning—too early to call on Brod. Impatiently, he stomped up and down the street until eight o'clock, which he judged to be the earliest decent hour for a call. "I've been thinking," he announced to the half-awake Brod. "If you'll take me on, everything will follow; if not—nothing; I'll be exactly where I was before." No promises, no terms, no contracts—just the cards on the table; the composer was leaving himself open to the most ruthless exploitation. Yet he seemed to know instinctively that this was the right approach. Brod had many commitments just then and was not at all anxious to take on another. It was precisely Janáček's disingenuousness and naiveté that Brod found so disarming. He would see what he could do. "In for a penny, in for a pound!" cried Janáček cheerfully. Very well, said Brod, he would think about taking on the job of translating the libretto; he did not know that he could do much more for the time being.

Leoš Janáček (above) and Max Brod at the time of their first collaboration.

As it turned out, he was to do a great deal more. Twelve years earlier, Mahler's interest in a possible Viennese production had come to nought because no German translation had been available. Now Mahler was dead and a new crew was in charge in Vienna: the conductor Hugo Reichenberger, manager Hans Gregor (who was also active as stage director), and chief stage director Wilhelm von Wymetal. Still, nothing could be done without a German text. Janáček had one well-wisher in Vienna, Emil Hertzka, the editor-in-chief of the great music publishing house Universal Edition, which had been founded in 1901; the two men had met because both served on Austria-Hungary's central committee for folk music. At Brod's urging, Hertzka expressed a cautious interest in publishing *Jenufa* once a German version was available, and in letting Universal Edition represent the composer abroad—always provided that Brod's translation was acceptable. Of course sales would be much greater if the opera could be meanwhile produced in Vienna, and perhaps in Berlin as well. Hertzka immediately began exerting himself in that direction. He became, so to speak, a volunteer press agent for the opera even before he had definitely agreed to become Janáček's publisher. He urged Brod to send him his translation of each act as it was finished. His plan was to have the German text inked into the previously published Czech piano score and to submit it to the Vienna opera in that form.

To be sure, Universal Edition in Vienna was not the only fish in the sea; nor was Brod the only one to take an interest in Janáček. Apart from local firms in Brno and Prague (mainly patriotic nonprofit associations devoted to the advancement of Czech music), German publishers also rose to the bait. They were egged on by Brod's attorney Jan Löwenbach, who occasionally served as his agent and now took it upon himself to act also on behalf of Janáček, whom he admired extravagantly. Löwenbach was a specialist in copyright law whose entire free time was devoted to music—as translator, librettist, organizer, contributor to music journals, and in general a tireless enthusiast who became one of the founders of the Ochranné Sdružení Autorské (an authors' and composers' protective society whose bylaws he set up) and mainstay of the Czechoslovak section of the International Society for Contemporary Music. It is in fact evi-

dent from materials that surfaced after the Second World War
that it was Löwenbach who brought Janáček to Brod's attention.
When the Nazis occupied Czechoslovakia in 1939, Löwenbach
escaped to England and later moved to New York, where he died
in 1972; his papers are in the special collections of the California
State University at San Diego, in the keeping of musicologist
Jaroslav Mráček, who is of Czech origin. Just before he left
Prague, Löwenbach made up a bundle of letters that ultimately
wound up in the archives of the National Museum, where they
were discovered after the war. (They are now in the museum's
literary archives at Strahov, under Signature S 64.) The Janáček–
Löwenbach correspondence was edited by Ivo Stolařík and published in a slim volume by the music section of the Silesian Studies Institute in Opava in 1958. Stolařík acknowledges Brod's aid
in assembling the correspondence. Neither Löwenbach nor Stolařík are mentioned in Brod's autobiography, even though it was
Löwenbach who negotiated Brod's first contract with Hertzka—
a translation of another Czech libretto, of an opera by Vítězslav
Novák, in 1915—and even though the two men later collaborated
on a libretto of an opera by Jaroslav Křička based on Oscar
Wilde's "The Canterville Ghost." (It is a comical short story in
which the family of the U.S. minister, called Mr. Hollywood in
this updated version, brings about the banishment and final release of the specter that haunts their country house.) Löwenbach
must have suggested the translation of *Jenufa* to Brod, for Stolařík reproduces a reply written a few days after Brod's first
review of *Jenufa* appeared in *Schaubühne*.

BROD TO LÖWENBACH, 27 NOVEMBER 1916

I can't decide for the present. In any case I am very glad
that you make such a case for Janáček. I'll be able to let you
have my answer in about two weeks, as I am in over my head
at present.

P.S. Director Hertzka queried me just today about the same
thing.

Brod's letter inviting Janáček to visit him is dated a day later,
so it is indeed likely that it was Löwenbach who first suggested

the translation job to Brod. Moreover, the materials at San Diego contain a draft of a letter from Mrs. Löwenbach (to the Czech musicologist Kateřina Šulcová-Holásková, written in the 1960s) in which she recalls that Brod sent her husband a post-card—unfortunately lost—worded approximately as follows: "Under the overwhelming impression of Janáček's personality I have decided to translate *Její pastorkyňa.*"

Why did Löwenbach not attempt the translation himself? Stolařík says it was because he found the task too daunting. He wrote of Löwenbach,

> As a great admirer of this Janáček work he had an interest in having it reach the Vienna as well as some German stage as rapidly as possible, and—even though he was himself a trans-lator of Czech songs and folk songs into German—he wanted Dr. Max Brod to translate *Jenufa.* With his proverbial modesty and critical sense he was too diffident to translate *Jenufa.* He regarded Dr. Brod as the ideal translator of Janáček's work be-cause that writer and poet was himself not only a composer of vocal and dramatic music, but also a linguist who had mastered the German dialects and could thus render the various idiomatic nuances of the libretto.

This note suggests that Löwenbach did indeed play a larger role at the beginning than has previously been ascribed to him. There can be no doubt that he later helped Janáček considerably, especially through his contacts with America, but his next shot went wide of the mark. He attempted to interest the great German music publisher B. Schotts Söhne in Mainz in *Jenufa,* although he knew that Brod was even then negotiating with Hertzka, whom Löwenbach did not altogether trust.

Löwenbach sent Schott a proposal on 27 November 1916, with which he enclosed a copy of the *Schaubühne* review by Brod, whom he proposed as a translator; and under separate cover he sent the piano score. The firm immediately expressed its interest—even before the score had arrived—but would make no definite commitment until a translation (or at least a sum-mary) of the libretto was in hand. Löwenbach then took it upon himself to wire an invitation to Schott's representative to the next performance of *Jenufa* and also asked Janáček to hold off signing a contract with Universal Edition; what was the hurry, since Brod would not even start on the translation until January, anyway? Janáček was inclined to stick with Hertzka, whom he knew in person and whose office in Vienna was nearer to Brno than Schott's in Mainz, but he declared himself willing to wait just a little, especially after Löwenbach had pointed out that Schott's offer would be somewhat more advantageous and that Schott was better situated to place the work in Germany and in other countries than a Viennese firm was. Schott's representative never made it to Prague—he had been held up because he could not get a passport so quickly in wartime—but declared the firm's readiness to consider any other works that Janáček might have in manuscript. Löwenbach was delighted. What about *Mister Brouček's Excursion to the Moon*? Or a work for soloists, mixed choir, and orchestra that Janáček had completed in 1914, *Eternal Gospel*, which was about to have its première in Prague? (The two compositions were based on the works of the two most important Czech poets of their day: *Brouček* on the satire by Svatopluk Čech, the leading exponent of a native literary style; and *Eternal Gospel* on a poem by the more cosmopolitan Jaroslav Vrchlický, who sought to relate Czech literature to the mainstream of European tradition.) Schott liked *Eternal Gospel,* but in the end nothing came of these negotiations, either. Hertzka declared himself ready to meet any other firm's terms. The deal with Universal Edition was clinched after an unexpected development at the beginning of 1917.

The German opera house in Prague was putting on a double bill of two contemporary one-acters, the world première of the opera *Florentinische Tragödie* (A Florentine Tragedy) by its chief conductor Alexander von Zemlinsky and a work by the Viennese critic and composer Julius Bittner, *Höllisch Gold* (Hell's Gold), which Universal Edition had published. An excursion to Prague was organized: Hertzka, Reichenberger, Bittner, and another critic, Richard Specht of the *Illustriertes Wiener Extrablatt*. If they could catch a performance of *Jenufa* during their stay in Prague, Hertzka could kill three birds with one stone. Reichenberger would hear and see the work and might be persuaded to recommend its staging in Vienna; Bittner and Specht would doubtless publish reviews in Vienna; and, based on their reactions, Hertzka could come to a final publishing decision. The proposed trip was less than three weeks off. Could an extra performance of *Jenufa* be scheduled at the National Theater on such short notice?

It could and it was. It would have to be a Sunday matinée on 4 March 1917, the same day as the two one-acters—the gentlemen from Vienna would get their fill of modern opera that day—but that could not be helped. Hertzka and Bittner shared a box with Brod that afternoon. Bittner made critical remarks throughout the first act, until Brod began to think gloomily that Hertzka would lose heart and decide against publishing the score—a fear that was intensified when Hertzka remarked, during the first intermission, that surely no European opera audience would accept a barbaric episode such as a baby's murder. (This in the midst of a war that cost thirteen million dead, and just after the German high command had declared unrestricted submarine warfare.) When Bittner's critical asides continued after the intermission, Brod angrily slammed out of the box.

This instinctive act proved to be decisive. Hertzka telephoned the next morning to offer a publishing contract. The reviews in the Vienna papers were not unfavorable. Reichenberger recommended a performance in Vienna. (He also recommended Zemlinsky's *Florentine Tragedy*; it was accepted and performed—and failed.) But a recommendation was not enough. More powerful forces now intervened.

Franz Josef I, the aged emperor-king, had died in 1916. Because his crown prince had shot himself or had been shot at Mayerling and his heir apparent had been shot at Sarajevo, the throne went to his grandnephew Charles, who was still in his twenties. The war was not going at all well for Austria-Hungary. Charles secretly sought to negotiate a separate peace with the Allies and to hold his crumbling realm together. The Dual Monarchy had been formed fifty years before, after the Prussian defeat, when Hungary had been given greater autonomy, including a separate parliament. Yet that left the Slav, Italian, and other minorities more dissatisfied than ever. At the eleventh hour, the young emperor tried to strengthen Austria's position by a more conciliatory policy toward these minorities, especially the Czechs. But that did not please some of his German-speaking subjects, who wished for a stronger alignment with Germany and advocated a harder line. In the resulting wrangles, even cultural events assumed a political significance. A Vienna première of a new Czech opera would please the court—it would be viewed as a conciliatory gesture—but not the hard-liners.

In this atmosphere, stronger measures than Reichenberger's recommendation were called for. Janáček, who was growing more sophisticated under the worldly Gabriela's guidance, asked Schmoranz whether one might persuade Otakar Trnka (the name means blackthorn), a Czech engineer who as minister of public works was a member of the imperial cabinet, to take an interest in the proposed production. Schmoranz thought it quite feasible. But first Brod's translation would have to be completed—and accepted.

A new complication now arose. Reichenberger viewed *Jenufa* as a folkloristic piece of verismo, a notion diametrically opposed to Janáček's conception of the work. To be sure, the voice parts were in a dialect that occasionally departed from the invariable first-syllable accentuation of standard Czech, and Janáček had taken other liberties besides to approximate ordinary speech (which was doubtless a factor in the work's long travail at the hands of the "literary" Prague purists). Reichenberger decided these subtleties could be best rendered if the work were set in some Austrian regional dialect, Tyrolean for choice, which would have had an unintended comic effect, like doing an English *Cavalleria rusticana* in a Lancashire accent. Brod fought like a lion against every change in his carefully wrought and expert translation, to the point of imperiling the work's acceptance, but in the end had to yield part of the way, especially since he dreaded the other extreme even more—setting the text in a sort of stilted "operatic" language he called *Operndeutsch*. Hertzka tried to mediate between Brod and Reichenberger. He urged Brod to accept at least some of the changes—they could always be restored in the printed edition—and at the same time gave Reichenberger a small honorarium for his "corrections" and accepted some songs of his for publication. (Brod won in the end: the printed libretto followed his translation verbatim, and the piano score was rid of Reichenberger's changes in the second edition.)

Still the Vienna première was not assured. Months had passed since the special matinée in Prague; the 1916–17 season had ended without a decision. The delay was hard on Janáček, too. *Jenufa* was not the only work he worried about; there were also the two parts of his satiric *Mister Brouček's Excursions,* about which the energetic Löwenbach was negotiating on his own hook with still another German firm, Drei Masken Verlag, which had expressed an interest in *Brouček* and had asked to see a German libretto. Löwenbach had sent off *Mister Brouček's Excursion to the Moon* to the publisher without checking with Janáček first, who had meanwhile completed the second part, *Mister Brouček's Excursion into the Fifteenth Century.* Janáček complained about it to Gabriela.

JANÁČEK TO GABRIELA HORVÁTOVÁ, 29 DECEMBER 1917

. . . Dr. Löwenbach writes that Drei Maskenverlag of Berlin are taking an interest in me. And the luckless man has sent them, without my permission, the proofs of the [Czech] piano score of *Brouček*; and he doesn't even know it has turned into a bilogy!

This negotiation proved fruitless, too.

Finally, well into the 1917–18 season, *Jenufa* was scheduled for early in the new year. Meanwhile, a new possibility had arisen. After the Prague première, and after Gabriela Horvátová had shown her the piano score at Janáček's urging, the renowned soprano Emmy Destinn had expressed an interest in singing the title part in Prague. Hertzka was agog with excitement. Once the world-famous singer learned Jenufa for Prague, she might be willing to sing it in Vienna, in Berlin, in—who knows?—New York after the war; had she not created the role of Minnie for the 1910 world première of Puccini's *Girl of the Golden West* at the Metropolitan? The Czech-born soprano (her real name was Ema Věra Kittlová) had sung in New York during several seasons beginning with 1908, but had been kept in Europe by the war. She went through the part with the assistant conductor Vincenc Maixner, who was coaching her for some other roles. She asked for more time. A year later she still had Janáček on tenterhooks: she wrote him, "Your temperamental style is—forgive me—devilishly difficult." She never did sing Jenufa—in fact, she never sang any Czech operas at all except the works of Smetana and Fibich's *Šárka* (perhaps to avoid being typed abroad) and no modern operas except Puccini's—which led her biographer, Artuš Rektorys, to exclaim ruefully, "How much greater would have been Destinn's artistic significance had she mastered *Jenufa* instead of *The Girl of the Golden West* and had she not let herself be robbed of the glory of the worldwide success of this work of Janáček's by the great achievement of another international artist of Czech origin—Maria Jeritza!"

For that was who had been selected for the title role in the Vienna opera house: its most glamorous and accomplished lyric soprano, born in Brno (and no less distinguished than Emmy Destinn: she had been Richard Strauss's first *Ariadne* in 1912 and was to go on to a brilliant career at the Metropolitan after the war). Her real name was Jedliczka, and she spoke and corresponded with Janáček in German, although she knew Czech well enough to sing in that language in Prague. In the part of Kostelnička, Reichenberger cast a regular member of the Vienna opera, Lucy Weidt. (She would find the role so exhausting that she would ask for and get a month's leave after six performances, which meant that the work would have to be dropped from the repertory for a while; Brod's suggestion that Janáček should then ask Vienna to borrow Gabriela Horvátová from Prague was not taken up.)

At last *Jenufa* was in rehearsal. Then, with little more than two weeks to go, a bolt out of the blue. On 29 January 1918 three ultras in the imperial parliament—Hans Schürff, Leopold Waber, and Othmar Wedra—put a formal question to the minister of ecclesiastical affairs and public instruction (the official in charge of state theaters). How had it come about, they asked, that the Vienna Opera had scheduled no fewer than nine non-German operas in the short span between January 22 and February 3, and was moreover preparing to produce, at great expense and with much ado, the new work of some Czech, in which both words and music followed a narrowly Czech nationalistic concept? Surely this was not the time for the imperial and royal court opera of the capital and residence city of Vienna to take such an unpatriotic stand, just when the Czech leaders had unleashed their sharpest political campaign yet. Would not the minister intervene in this favoritism toward the composers of other nationalities and put an end to the proposed production, which was nothing but a provocation of Vienna's German population?

If such an intervention had been proposed three years earlier, the première might have been canceled. At the beginning of the war a few disaffected Czech units had gone over to the Russians—one regiment defected en masse, with its officers—and public opinion was not favorably inclined toward Czech national aspirations. But now, in the war's fourth year, the mood had changed, and a spirit of "we're all in this together" prevailed. Besides, the young emperor was trying to set a new tone, one that did not favor a reactionary chauvinism. To stop the intervention in its tracks, he announced that he and his empress would attend the première, which automatically made it a command performance: the bills would be inscribed *Auf allerhöchsten Befehl* (By Supreme Command).

With excitement in musical circles mounting, Janáček and Brod traveled to Vienna. (Brod usually stayed at the Hotel Graben, which now boasts a historical marker attesting that he and Kafka repeatedly stayed there.) Brod was still fighting for restorations of his text. Janáček lent a hand with the rehearsals; at one point he even took the ballet through the first-act dances. Earlier, he had asked the stage director, Wilhelm von Wymetal, to let the company's ballet master come to Prague so that he could see these dances for himself in authentic execution. Not a chance, said Wymetal; besides, what did it matter, since the Viennese audiences did not know one Czech dance from another? Janáček was incensed at this cynicism but tried to save the situation by asking the Prague basso Robert Polák, who was also a painter, to sketch some of the steps for the Viennese colleagues. Nothing came of that, either; and now it was too late. In fact, the staging also left much to be desired, and Reichenberger's tempi reflected his attitude that he knew his business better than some yokel musician from the provinces.

Brod and Janáček shared a box at the première, which took place on 16 February 1918. Whenever anything on the stage or in the orchestra was not to Janáček's liking, he poked an elbow into Brod's ribs. By the end of the first act, Brod reports, all his poor ribs were sore. Brod wrote:

> Staging and performance went wrong even though a good deal of effort had gone into the production and the cast was first class (with Jeritza in the title role). The conductor dragged out the great first-act ensemble ("Every couple must live through its painful time of sorrow") to twice its length. Renewed pokes in my ribs. A high point in this regard was the entrance of Kostelnička, another much admired singer; I believe she was the company's Brünnhilde. Janáček's librettist (Gabriela Preissová) had taken this character directly from Moravian village life, a royal figure, a sort of Deborah, a woman elder to whom the entire village looks up with respect and who accordingly appears in her Sunday best (it is a holiday), carrying a beautiful lace shawl over her arm as is the custom. The villagers kiss her hand. Janáček often told me how he had once made a tour of southern Moravia with Rodin and how the sculptor had been overcome with admiration at the noble and distinguished bearing of these village elders. And what was the Vienna opera's interpretation of this character? Kostelnička appeared in a soiled everyday dress, quasi "realistic" (but in reality totally wrong), with a rake over her shoulder. I looked at Janáček at that moment. His face was distorted with pain; he was crying.

The evening was nevertheless a great success, although Their Majesties did not show after all. (The management had been asked whether the opera's plot was at all exciting; upon learning that it was, the royal pair had bowed out—the prolific young empress, Zita, was once again in an interesting condition and wanted to take no chances.) Janáček had to take twenty curtain calls. The reviews were generally favorable, with two exceptions. One was the review by Julius Korngold, who had succeeded Eduard Hanslick in 1902 as music critic of the influential *Neue freie Presse* and who was the father of another composer, Erich Korngold, then a promising lad of twenty. Julius Korngold had gone to the trouble of writing Löwenbach for published materials about Janáček, which were duly sent him. In private conversation, Korngold said that *Jenufa* had greatly impressed him. His review admitted that the work was effective in parts but con-

220481

cluded that the composer lacked the power of melodic invention. (Nevertheless, the piece was included in Korngold's collection of feuilletons *Die romanische Oper der Gegenwart* in 1922.) The other negative review appeared in the *Fremdenblatt*. Its reviewer, Richard Batka, had been active in Prague as music editor of the arts monthly *Kunstwart*; he was a confirmed Wagnerian. (Brod knew him—it was a music supplement in that journal that had awakened his enthusiasm for Carl Nielsen.) Now Batka held a more important post, although not quite top drawer by Vienna standards. Because of his earlier activity in Prague, he was supposed to be more knowledgeable about Czech music and musicians than his fellow critics and may have seized on the *Jenufa* première as his chance to show off by expressing some reservations.

The great hopes that Janáček and Brod had placed on the Vienna production were only partially fulfilled. The publication of a German version of *Jenufa* doubtless made a great difference to Janáček's future reputation, as did the fact that a great star, Maria Jeritza, had made the title role her own. For the rest, uncertain times were ahead. Before the year was out the war ended. Vienna ceased to be the glittering center of the Dual Monarchy and became the overgrown capital of a top-heavy republic the size of Ireland. The relative importance of music in the city's life did not change, but the absolute scale shrank considerably. After 1918 the Vienna Opera—now styled the *Staatsoper*—was to set aside *Jenufa* for seven years. Janáček's international reputation would have to ripen in other vineyards.

Although Janáček had decided to stick with Universal Edition in the end, he was quite flattered to have been the subject of negotiations with two other foreign publishing houses, even before the Vienna première of *Jenufa* and years before the world première of *Brouček*. For that did not take place until after the war, in Prague, on 23 April 1920, under the musical direction of Kovařovic's successor, Otakar Ostrčil, to whose care the ailing Kovařovic had entrusted the work as a first assignment. The delays were caused in part by wartime shortages—there was much correspondence about the lack of *širtink* ("shirting," a lightweight cotton fabric needed in great quantities to create an ethereal effect in the moon scenes)—but also by a near rebellion among the National Theater's principal singers, some of whose parts lay uncomfortably high. Janáček undertook to make the requisite changes himself, some of them even after the first performance—unlike the *Jenufa* rearrangements, which had been made by Kovařovic. (The *Jenufa* revisions, mainly changes in instrumentation and deletions of repetitive passages that Janáček bitterly resented at first, were generally conceded to have actually improved the work's effectiveness and were incorporated in the published versions; however, recent performances of the original version in Britain and France have been well received.) But *Mister Brouček's Excursions* never did become part of the Janáček canon. It is also his only major vocal work that Brod did not translate into German. He proffered advice on how to sharpen the satire and tighten the dramatic line, but he was a confirmed pacifist and thought that some of the fifteenth-century scenes glorified war—a bit of righteousness he ended by regretting.

In any case, it is abundantly clear that Janáček's hatred of Austrian rule and of insistence on German as the official language did not extend to publishing houses or opera companies. The Bohemian lands form a salient into German-speaking territory, cradle of much that is great in music and full of goodly prospects for aspiring artists. It had been quite obvious from the time of the Stamitzes, the Bendas, and the Dusíks (Dusseks), all the way to Hanslick and Korngold and Mahler that (to paraphrase Dr. Johnson) the noblest prospect which a Bohemian musician ever saw was the high road that led him to Berlin or Vienna. For opera composers, the road was blocked without a German translation; instances of Czech librettists being first translated into a language other than German must be rare indeed. (Brod was well versed in their problems; one of his last works, published in 1962, was a biographical novel about Karel Sabina, the librettist for Smetana's *Bartered Bride,* who was accused—wrongfully, in Brod's view—by his compatriots of being an Austrian informer.) Janáček knew full well what he owed to Brod, whose role extended far beyond that of a mere translator. "At the right moment he came along like a messenger from heaven," wrote Janáček. "Himself a poet. I am afraid to read my fill of his stirring words. They could lead me into vainglory."

Anni mirabiles

The decade that followed the end of the war in 1918 was an incredibly productive one for Janáček. His first successes in the wider world had greatly bucked him up. Czechoslovakia's newly won independence provided the additional incentives of rising national pride and higher visibility. He composed steadily: four more operas, a mass, several symphonic works, two string quartets—all destined to remain in the international repertory to the present day. Yet anyone seeking the main inspiration for this astonishing outburst of creativity had best look to the well-worn advice, *cherchez la femme.*

She was Kamila Stössl, a curly-headed and black-eyed charmer who was married to a businessman in Písek, a small market town in southern Bohemia. Janáček met her at a spa during the summer of 1917, when she was twenty-five and he was sixty-three. Their first contacts were prosaic enough: her ailing husband, whose wartime military service was limited to the home front, somehow contrived to supplement the meager rations available to the town-bound Janáček household by scrounging around the countryside for food.

There is no record of what his erstwhile love Gabriela Horvátová thought of her admirer's new acquaintance, but it is not difficult to surmise. The only surviving references in their correspondence speak of the tasty windfalls to come his way. "Goose liver today, enough to fill a pot," he writes Gabriela on 10 January 1918, for all the world like Mr. Pickwick inscribing the fateful note to Mrs. Bardell; "I brought home the bacon and butter from the Stössls. Some venison. A rabbit came hopping

Kamila Stössl.

our way, too, with a bit of bacon tied to his foot!" The next day, there is a terse rebuke to who knows what impertinence—although he was not above enjoying a piece of irreverent gossip on other occasions: "The Stössls are honest people and there's no call to malign them." After that the letters cool off rapidly. There is one more spark three months later, after the Vienna première of *Jenufa*, when Janáček writes Gabriela apologetically (on 23 April 1918), "I wrote you a tender yearning letter yesterday. [That letter is also missing from the archives.] Do not wonder at it, let no one wonder: it is our natural lot, ardent and inflamed composers that we are. We can't help it." The last letter is dated two months later; then the correspondence breaks off, except for a brief note of congratulation written fully ten years afterward, in 1928, on the completion of her twenty-fifth year with the National Theater, in which Janáček addresses her formally by the equivalent of "Dear Madam" and commends her for her "brilliant performance of years ago in the role of Kostelnička."

There can be no doubt that Kamila Stössl became not only the great love of Janáček's life but also a creature of fantasy to whose realm he soared in his imagination, like Mister Brouček to the moon, to escape the commonplaces of the workaday world. No matter that he remained married to Zdenka, who knew all about Kamila; no matter that the affair was possibly never consummated—that his deep feelings were not even reciprocated. To be sure, Kamila was not cut out to be the object of devout worship and yearning reveries; she could scarcely be cast as Beatrice to Janáček's Dante. She was the down-to-earth wife of a merchant in a provincial town at some distance from Brno, the mother of two little boys, a merry and temperamental creature around whom Janáček's imagination spun a web of fancy that was worlds away from everyday life. He never wavered in his devotion to her. "We are bound together by a world of beauty alone—and all, all only imagined!" he wrote her in the tenth year of their friendship. "Yet in my life this imagined world is as vital as air and water to me."

Janáček's feelings for Kamila were repeatedly transfigured into expressions of the highest art. She was the direct inspiration for his heroines. But he also remained true to his progressive ideals. His heroes might alternate, like Tannhäuser, between erotic and sublime love; yet Kamila, translated to the stage, became neither a voluptuous Venus nor an angelic Elisabeth. Like Ibsen and Shaw—and Tolstoy, in his *Kreutzer Sonata*—Janáček came back again and again to the most modern of themes: a woman's right to follow her own heart in making her life's choices. Through the characters based on Kamila, his works came to figure as milestones on the road to the great moral revolution of his day.

The first outcome of this preoccupation was the song cycle *Diary of a Vanished Man* for tenor, mezzo-soprano, three-woman chorus, and piano. It is the setting of two groups of poems describing the plight of a prosperous peasant's son who is seduced by a gypsy girl, Zefka (Josephine), and abandons his home and inheritance for her when she bears him a son; he leaves behind only a notebook containing the poems. Janáček did nothing to clear up the matter of the poems' provenance. They were originally published anonymously in the Brno paper *Lidové noviny,* whose literary editor loved to mystify his public. (They are now believed to have been a hoax perpetrated by the Moravian writer and folklorist Jan Misárek.) But he left no doubt that the musical setting was inspired by Kamila. "I thought of you constantly while I composed it," he wrote her later. "You were my Zefka." He wanted her likeness, with her dark hair untied, to appear on the cover; and her stylized portrait did in fact become part of the design. But even after the *Jenufa* triumphs in Prague and Vienna and the flurry of interest in *Brouček,* publication of Janáček's further works was by no means a foregone conclusion. The *Diary* was completed in 1919; it was first performed in 1921 and published in the same year, in Brno. It was the second work to be translated by Max Brod.

His continuing championship of Janáček and their increasing collaboration may be traced in their voluminous correspondence, which forms the largest and most complete corpus of letters in the Janáček archives. (Janáček wrote in Czech, Brod in German.) If their friendship had flourished twenty years later, the correspondence might not have come into being, as they might have then availed themselves of the telephone. But the war of 1914–1918 had impeded European development of long-distance

ZÁPISNÍK
ZMIZELÉHO.

LEOŠ JANÁČEK.

VYDAL
OL PAZDÍREK, HUD. NAKLAD. v BRNĚ.

Title page of *Diary of a Vanished Man*. The female figure was meant to be a stylized likeness of Kamila Stössl, in accordance with Janáček's wish.

telephony. It is to that historical accident that we owe this rich source of information. Jan Racek, who prepared the original edition (volume nine in the publications from the Janáček archives), characterizes it as indispensable:

> Janáček's letters to Brod are materials of absolutely unique documentary value in throwing light on Janáček's final and most creative period. We have here a coherent and extensive set of written documents that form a reliable basis on which to found an understanding of Janáček's creative method and psychology, as well as of the artistic development of his work. Janáček the artist and Janáček the man could fully rely on Brod's support, particularly in view of his total dependability and devotion. He soon saw how Brod could take a selfless, partisan, fighting stance on behalf of his work and systematically promote it. Janáček's letters attest to an uncommon and ardent friendship between the Moravian master and his much younger collaborator, the more so since Janáček could count on Brod's absolute discretion. That is also why Janáček is so open and candid, cordial, and informative in these letters. Janáček often confides ideas in them that are for the most part entirely singular manifestations of his idiosyncratic artistic personality, ideas he expressed to none of his Czech friends. The portrait of Janáček's human and artistic personality is brilliantly rounded off and made whole by the inclusion of new and important traits.

In their first postwar letters, they commiserate about Hertzka in Vienna (both had had their misunderstandings with the publisher) and exchange cuttings about the successful German première of *Jenufa,* which took place on 16 November 1918—the week the war ended—in Cologne; Otto Klemperer was the conductor. (So much for the stab-in-the back theory, according to which it was the complete collapse of the home front that led to the defeat of the German armies.) Both men found themselves immersed in public life as the new Czechoslovak republic set about to form institutions appropriate to an independent state. Brod became for a time a member of the government press bureau. Janáček's Organ School became the Brno Conservatory of Music, but he was not appointed its principal: he was too near retirement age as these things are reckoned by academic bureaucrats. As a consolation prize, he was named professor of composition at the Prague Conservatory—largely an honorific appointment, since he continued to live in Brno.

Brod's political activities plunged him into despair. He had thought imperialism had been vanquished with the transformation of the Central Powers into democratic republics, only to find that it was rife among the victorious Allies, too. In the end it was Janáček who had to console him.

JANÁČEK TO BROD, 18 JANUARY 1919

I read about you often.

The printing of *Brouček* is done; I'll tell Hertzka to send you a copy of the piano score.

He is already making contacts in Italy and in America with regard to *Jenufa*.

Our legionnaires [Czechs and Slovaks who had fought on the side of the Allies] returning from Italy, France, and Russia tell me they read all about the Vienna première in the papers there.

Yet the Nat. Theater in Prague puts on nothing but Smetana for gala performances!

They push *Louise* under the French ambassador's nose. Surely he knows it better from Paris. After all, it is with *us* he should become acquainted here, not France!

We need *our own* country for our entire cultural life, including the arts. Not only to foster economic productivity but also our own artistic productivity.

Keep well and don't lose hope for the future. I believe in a happy one!

In May 1919 the Cologne opera put on *Jenufa* again. The city had been occupied by the British since the war's end; perhaps the music lovers among them would come to hear the opera and send word home. Meanwhile, wrote Brod, how about Copenhagen? Carl Nielsen had reopened their prewar correspondence and had sent him his richly scored fourth symphony ("The Inextinguishable"); would Janáček like to look over the score and perhaps recommend a Brno performance? Brod thought there was a spiritual relationship between the two composers; for all he knew a quid pro quo might be arranged. Janáček replied at once.

JANÁČEK TO BROD, 31 MAY 1919

I was glad to receive your note.
I'll stop by to see you on my next visit; it will be soon. I'll
pick up Nielsen's score then.
[František] Neumann is the chief of the Brno opera; he likes
to conduct concerts. I will put in a good word. . . .

His word would have been heeded, since Neumann owed his
appointment to Janáček; but the exchange did not come about.
(Janáček did not actually see the score until two years later, when
he judged the piece to be harsh and primitive.) Instead, *Jenufa*
would soon travel to Breslau, as Brod learned from a chance
meeting with his old school friend Lothar Wallerstein, the stage
director there (and later in Vienna and Salzburg). On the other
hand, Brod was skeptical about the chances of success of *Mister
Brouček's Excursions* in Germany, if only because the second
part celebrated the victory of a Bohemian army over a German
foe. Maybe a French version would fare better? And what about
a translation of a nice selection of Janáček's choral works into
German? Brod would be interested in doing that. (This project
was later realized.)

The fact was that Janáček was busy with an entirely new
project. He must have recognized that his talents were not suited
to arch satire after the indifferent reception of *Brouček*; and for
the moment he was not interested in writing purely instrumental
music. Even *The Diary of a Vanished Man* was highly programmatic. Although it was intended for concert performance, Janáček specified in some detail how it should be "staged," down to
suggestions for lighting the concert hall and for the alto's entrance and exit. Another opera, then; but on what theme? A
Slavonic one, that much was certain. In 1907 he had considered
Tolstoy's *Anna Karenina* for a libretto; in 1916, his play *A Living
Corpse*. Janáček went so far as to sketch an opening scene, then
abandoned the idea. (The story resembles that of *The Diary of
a Vanished Man* in that the chief protagonist leaves hearth and
home for a gypsy, but Tolstoy's hero, a drunkard who pretends
to commit suicide so that his wife may remarry, ends badly: he
is driven to actual suicide.) Janáček's friends helped in the
search. Václav Jiřikovský, one of the directors of the Brno thea-

ter, proposed several plays and finally staged one of them especially for Janáček, *The Storm* by the popular Russian playwright Aleksander Ostrovsky (whose *Snow Maiden* had been adapted as an opera by Rimsky-Korsakov). Janáček was very much taken with it and went to work on it at once. To be sure, substantial changes would be needed, in addition to the usual condensation. For a start, the title seemed unsatisfactory, since it had been used for several other pieces. Perhaps the heroine's name would be better. Even after he had finished the opera, Janáček was still fussing about what to call it.

JANÁČEK TO KAMILA STÖSSL, 6 MARCH 1921

After unusually hard toil I am done with my newest opera. I don't know whether to call it *The Storm* or *Catherine*. What weighs against *The Storm* is that there is already an opera by that title; against *Catherine,* that I'll be said to compose nothing but "women"! Jenufa—Catherine. I might as well have done with it and put three asterisks in place of the title $_*^{**}$.

The final title was suggested by Gustav Schmoranz: *Katya Kabanova* (Kát'a Kabanová in Czech), after Ostrovsky's heroine Katya (Cathy). The story is of a young wife who lives in a dull provincial town with an overbearing mother-in-law and a weakling husband; while he is away, she becomes involved with another man, but publicly confesses her sin after taking shelter in a ruined chapel during a storm, which she takes for a sign of divine wrath. (The Russian word for "storm," *groza,* also means "horror.") When the other man abandons her, she despairs and drowns herself in the Volga: a Russian Madame Bovary, created three years after Flaubert's original.

Janáček made many changes in Ostrovsky's text (translated into Czech by Vincenc Červinka) and ended by listing himself as the librettist. The work went so quickly—it was finished on 17 February 1921—that not a few inconsistencies crept into the plot that had to be fixed later, when Brod began to translate it into German.

Although the translation was made the same year that Janáček completed the opera, it was by no means the only project the two men had on their hands in 1921. For one thing, Janáček's earlier works were in demand after the initial success of *Jenufa*. In 1916 he had completed *Kašpar Rucký*, a burlesque (for soprano and women's chorus) about a seventeenth-century alchemist who commits suicide after he is exposed as a cheat and sentenced to death by quartering, but comes back to haunt the castle of his former patron, Emperor Rudolf II, for forty days. This work was first performed on 6 April 1921 by the Prague Women Teachers' Choir and became that group's greatest success during a subsequent tour of Germany. Brod was so impressed with it that he actually volunteered to undertake a translation, which was finished in time for the Czech publisher to set under the Czech text in the printed score. Brod had every confidence the work would succeed—more so than Janáček himself, who attended the première with some trepidation.

JANÁČEK TO BROD, 12 APRIL 1921

You have no idea how scared I was to come to Prague to hear *Kašpar Rucký*. I was afraid they wouldn't be able to manage it and would make an utter shambles of it! But it came off well.

I am sincerely grateful to you for your words of praise. They encourage me and strengthen my will to work. . . .

The Diary of a Vanished Man had its première in Brno the same month. Again Brod was on hand to review it; again he agreed to translate it right away. (This time there were to be three separate versions: a Czech and a German text printed under the music, and a French prose translation by Hanuš Jelínek on a separate page.) More and more, Janáček was coming to regard Brod as his confidant and fellow conspirator. What would Brod think of involving the government in subsidizing Czechoslovak arts abroad? And how would one go about it? As a journalist and member of the cabinet press bureau, Brod presumably knew all about such things; hadn't he introduced Janáček to some of the officials?

JANÁČEK TO BROD, 31 MAY 1921

I had an interesting letter from dir. Hertzka today. He complains that the Czechoslovak republic's embassies do nothing to promote Czech music.

He advises me that Mr. Bamboschek has been named principal conductor of the Metropol. Opera in New York for next season. According to his name he must be Czech. [Actually, he came from Trieste.] Haven't we any contacts with him?

Wouldn't it be possible to influence him from *Prague*?

He [Hertzka] will send me the American papers that mention *Jenufa*.

What is to be done?

I think the following:

1. I know of no Czech publisher nor theatrical-operatic agency that could successfully act for us abroad.

2. Univ. Edition has an interest in me, in [Vítězslav] Novák, and in Suk.

3. *His objective evaluation: we are sadly lacking.* Everyone is still infatuated with Smetana's operas which—out with it, then, since we must—no longer accord with a modern view of opera.

4. Couldn't one get a *commission and a subvention* on the part of our government for Univ. Edition to promote Czech opera abroad?

5. Should I seek an audience with prime minister Černý in that connection?

Talk it over confidentially with the esteemed gentlemen whom I have had the honor of meeting and let me know what they would think of such a step.

Dr. Branberger [a Czech musicologist and Janáček's colleague at the Prague conservatory] came to Brno. But he looks *backward and not forward*.

The French translation of *The Diary of a Vanished Man* is supposed to be in Dr. Hanuš Jelínek's hands.

Do urge him along in this undertaking.

Brod did not think it likely that the government would subsidize a foreign firm but suggested that a letter to his chief at the press bureau, František Ebel, might do no harm, especially since he had great influence in musical circles and knew the conductor of the Czech Philharmonic, Václav Talich. Meanwhile, Brod could perhaps send a piece on Janáček to the Czechoslovak Press Bureau in Washington—that would further the cause in America! As to Jelínek, he might manage a French translation of *Diary* in prose, but there was no one in all Prague who could do it in verse, let alone verse that would fit the music; best not to hold up the printing and to settle for a prose translation for the time being, since there was no immediate prospect of a French performance, was there? (Actually, *Diary* had its Paris première the following year, in Czech; a French verse translation was ultimately provided by Daniel Muller.)

Brod's tireless efforts in promoting the music of Janáček, which included writing reviews for foreign publications, nudging music publishers, and generally keeping his name before the public, were the more remarkable since Brod feared they might keep him from what he saw as his real work: literary activity (as distinct from musical and journalistic pursuits). Nevertheless, during 1920 and 1921 alone he published a play, three political tracts, a volume of poems, a monograph about his former composition teacher Adolf Schreiber (who had drowned himself in a Berlin lake after his career had ground to a halt), and a massive two-volume work of philosophy and religion, *Heidentum, Christentum, Judentum* (Paganism, Christianity, Judaism). He also worked on a novel, *Franzi: Eine Liebe zweiten Ranges* (Franzi: A Love Affair of the Second Rank), and somehow—in between his job, his writing, and the various negotiations on Janáček's behalf—he finished a first draft in June 1921. At that point he managed to squeeze in a two-week vacation. No sooner was he back than Janáček was importuning him to undertake the translation of *Katya Kabanova,* for publication by Universal Edition. Brod agreed, provided the publisher would first formally commission the job. Hertzka obliged with a contract, and the work started.

It was not smooth sailing. The very first perfunctory glance revealed a syllable missing from the text. A few days later Brod was pointing out several incongruities in the plot to Janáček, who was apt to be a little careless in such things; besides, he had been in such a hurry to get on with the work that he had adapted Ostrovsky's play in some haste. Nevertheless, the first act was translated in less than three weeks and went off to Hertzka in Vienna. Janáček was in and out of Prague that autumn and winter—he had agreed to give a series of fortnightly lectures at the conservatory on a theme close to his heart, the development of music theory into an exact science—and he met several times with Brod to thrash out the remaining problems of *Katya Kabanova*. It would not be a verbatim translation by any means. In some instances Brod went back to Ostrovsky's original to add phrases that would make the Russian milieu more comprehensible to a non-Slav audience. Another worry was the accentuation of Russian names: Janáček had read them as a Czech would, with the stress on the first syllable, and Brod undertook to place them against the music so as to fit the Russian pronunciation. (In the same way, the gentle reader would doubtless visualize "Universal Edition" as two English words, whereas in German they are run together and are differently pronounced and stressed: ooniverZAALeditsiawn.) Even so, exactly one month after Brod had received the work, *Katja Kabanowa* (as the title was rendered in German) was finished. The two men were reading proofs six weeks later and final proofs a month after that (in January 1922). The piano score was published by Universal Edition in March 1922.

Brod's changes were gratefully accepted by Janáček. The Czech musicologist and conductor Jaroslav Vogel cites several instances of particularly felicitous improvements that Brod made and goes on to state unequivocally:

> All honor is due Max Brod for his acuteness in detecting and for his great skill in correcting [Janáček's] textual inadvertencies in his translation. . . . I think these examples serve to make it obvious what an exaggeration it is to insist that Janáček's every word is perfectly weighed and inalterable [as the Janáček specialist František Pala had asserted], and therefore how little basis there is for the consequences drawn from that.

Katya Kabanova was first performed in Brno, on 23 November 1921. Even before the Brno première, Ostrčil had accepted it for Prague. Brod published reviews in Prague and Berlin, and the work was on its way; it would undergo nothing like the travail that had attended *Jenufa,* despite the failure of *Brouček.* At long last, Janáček's circumstances eased somewhat. Besides royalties, he had the sinecure of a professorship at the State Conservatory in Prague; the Organ School in Brno, now also a State Conservatory, equipped a small house on its grounds for his residence; and when his brother František's widow decided to leave Hukvaldy, Janáček bought her cottage in his native village and for the first time became a householder. He furnished a sunny room as his study, complete with a harmonium at which he composed whenever he could get away, looking out at a small orchard and listening to a flock of chickens clucking and scratching away in the yard. It was in this rustic environment that his thoughts slowly turned to the idea of an opera about animals. But the external world also claimed him. An important event was in the offing that would greatly advance his international repute.

At the end of January 1922 Brod reported that the chief of the Berlin State Opera, Max von Schillings, was coming to Prague to conduct the Czech Philharmonic the following month. He might well want to choose a new Czech opera for Berlin. Several composers' well-wishers advanced their candidates. Schillings was predisposed toward *Jenufa,* which he knew about from Brod's writings but had never heard. (An unspoken consideration was that his good friend—and wife to be—Barbara Kemp would make a great Jenufa.) Could Janáček ask Ostrčil to schedule a performance on the day before the Philharmonic's concert? This performance was duly scheduled, and Janáček came to Prague to see the great man; they first met over tea at Brod's apartment.

Back home again in Brno, Janáček sat down to write his bread-and-butter letter.

JANÁČEK TO BROD, 23 FEBRUARY 1922

First of all my thanks for all your good work, running about, playing host, "diplomatic" negotiating. I think we gained an honest victory.

Schillings told me he has decided on *Jenufa.* He said he couldn't introduce works in Berlin whose style reflected world weariness, works of a sort of which Germany had aplenty. He invited me to come to Berlin in mid-March.

We'll see how matters develop further. I told Mr. Ostrčil quite openly about Schillings's intentions. He is an honest person. How did it go otherwise?

Brod went out of his way to urge Janáček to take up Schillings's invitation, even to the point of mentioning that the trip would not cost much, since Germany was in the throes of runaway inflation and Czechoslovak crowns would buy a lot of marks just then. (Czechoslovakia had escaped postwar inflation by a partial currency devaluation that had been resolutely—if somewhat inequitably—carried out by its brilliant first finance minister, Alois Rašín, who was later assassinated for his pains.) To his beloved Kamila, Janáček wrote in a similar vein, among a forest of exclamation points:

JANÁČEK TO KAMILA STÖSSL, 25 FEBRUARY 1922

I had a hot time of it during 19–22 February 1922 in Prague! The *Intendant* of the Berlin State Opera was making his selection of Czech operas in Prague! And well, he selected my *Jenufa*! How his head must have tingled during the selection! For they tried in every way to stop him from selecting that Janáček! I am off, soon I think, for Berlin. I'll see how this thing develops further. All sorts of political obstacles remain.

To deal with them, Brod now took up Janáček's earlier suggestion to seek government support. During a trip to attend the première of his fantasy drama *Die Fälscher* (Forgers) at the Neues Volkstheater in Berlin, Brod sought out Vlastimil Tusar, Czechoslovakia's ambassador to Germany, and persuaded him to receive Schillings, presumably to offer the embassy's aid in bringing about the *Jenufa* production. Would it help if the embassy would sponsor a concert of Czech music and include a work of Janáček's? How about some authentic peasant costumes for the cast? This intervention was evidently successful. Schillings penciled in *Jenufa* for the following autumn; the concert would take place just before the première; and Janáček would not have to travel to Berlin after all. (In the event, the concert came off on schedule on 21 September 1922 in Berlin's prestigious Bechstein Hall, with a program that included a highly successful performance of *The Diary of a Vanished Man,* but the opera was not staged for another eighteen months; the "political obstacles" proved to be more formidable than anyone had anticipated.)

With his prospects improving, Janáček had begun to think about another opera. He may have grown wary of librettos based on popular plays or novels; this time it would be an original theme. But what? *Katya Kabanova* had left him depleted, undecided. He puttered about in his bucolic retreat. He went on taking down his speech melodies, tried to measure the duration of tones only fractions of a second long by a gadget he had got from the Brno physicist Vladimír Novák (Hipp's "chronoscope," a clockwork mechanism with electromagnetically actuated pointers), wrote an airy newspaper article about it that even the patient Brod found exasperating to translate, and desultorily dipped into the physics literature himself. His announcement that the last bit of the *Katya Kabanova* score had gone off to Hertzka ends on an uncharacteristically languid note.

JANÁČEK TO BROD, 10 JANUARY 1922

So what now!
My head is a void, like a burnt-out shell. I don't know what to sink my teeth into.
I dabble in folk songs; I read Einstein the while. Yet his relativity of time and space is not suited to sound. We live by air, not the ether. Our fragrance is of the earth. But at least we stand on firm ground.
Keep well!

Yet he quickly revived when the subject for another opera turned up, from the same source that had yielded *The Diary of a Vanished Man*: the local newspaper, Brno's *Lidové noviny*. Its literary editor, always on the lookout for suitable original drawings, had found some in the Prague studio of the painter Stanislav Lolek, merry sketches of animals in the manner of the German poet-caricaturist Wilhelm Busch. Another staff member, Rudolf Těsnohlídek, was commissioned to compose some accompanying light verse. He decided to make a serial story of it instead, named for the chief character, *Liška Bystronožka* (Vixen Fleetfoot). A printer's error made it *Liška Bystrouška* (Vixen Sharpears), which was all the same to Těsnohlídek; he let it stand. (He could not have foreseen that the title of his

Kiplingesque *contes,* written for a provincial daily, would one day become a bone of contention among scholars and critics in several countries.)

The serial had appeared during 1920, while Janáček was working on *Katya Kabanova.* According to the recollections of the longtime family servant Marie Stejskalová (published in Prague in 1964), it was she who first drew Janáček's attention to the serial. He began to collect the installments. At a loose end in 1922, he asked Těsnohlídek to prepare a libretto, but the author begged off (even though he was to lend a hand with the final version). Janáček had to make up his own libretto, which he called *Příhody Lišky Bystroušky* (The Adventures of Vixen Bystrouška). He worked on it on and off during 1922, especially during a prolonged summer stay at Hukvaldy. By autumn he had the libretto; the music took another year or more. He finished a first version on 17 March 1923 but went on making changes while his copyist, Jaroslav Kulhánek, was preparing a fair copy. (Janáček made some of the changes verbally.) A final copy was not completed until 12 January 1924. It was during this period that he wrote Kamila Stössl his most melancholy letter.

JANÁČEK TO KAMILA STÖSSL, 3 APRIL 1923

. . . I work on Bystrouška as the devil catches flies—when he's got nothing else to do. I captured Bystrouška for the forest and the tristesse of declining years. . . .

The idea of animals as dramatis personae goes back at least twenty-five centuries to the fables of Aesop, from whom we get our view of the fox as a cunning animal, the Reynard of medieval European literature, Goethe's Reineke, all the way down to Stravinsky's burlesque *Renard* (1916). Maeterlinck had written about *The Life of the Bee* (1901); so had Waldemar Bonsels, in his *Adventures of Maya the Bee* (1912). Nearer home, the brothers Josef and Karel Čapek had just completed their satirical *Insect Play* (1921). But in Těsnohlídek's stories (and Janáček's libretto) animals share the action with people, and the eponymous central character is not a male fox but a vixen, symbol of Goethe's *Ewig-Weibliche* (that which is eternal in woman). In

other hands, the result could have easily sunk to mawkish sentimentality—one need only think of Felix Salten's similar juve-
nile, *Bambi,* which came out the same year. Instead, Janáček's
opera turned out to be his most charming and lyrical work, one
that occupies a position in his output similar to that of *Die Meis-
tersinger* in Wagner's or *Falstaff* in Verdi's.

The opera's nine dreamy episodes follow no particular logic,
which has perplexed all listeners (beginning with Brod) whose
thinking tends to be what later critics would call "linear." In the
first act the stodgy gamekeeper is woken from a forest nap by a
frog startled into jumping on him by the appearance of the young
Vixen; the gamekeeper catches her and ties her up with his dog,
who makes advances to her; she tries to run away when the gamekeeper's little boy teases her but is recaptured and finally escapes
after making a meal of a proud rooster whom she tempts into
venturing too near. In the second act, the homeless Vixen leads
the forest animals in harassing a badger, whom she finally pro-
vokes into yielding his lair to her by fouling it; his human counterpart, an old parson, comes to a country inn where an aging
bachelor schoolmaster is being so mercilessly badgered about his
youthful love for a girl called Veronica that he angrily stomps
off into the forest; inebriated, he trips and espies the Vixen
behind a sunflower, which he drunkenly takes for another long-
time love, Terynka; the old parson appears and also recalls a
youthful infatuation; then the gamekeeper comes by and aims a
shot at the Vixen but misses, while parson and schoolmaster
cower for their lives; she accepts the advances of a gallant male
fox, admits him to her lair with the usual consequences, and a
wedding is hastily arranged. In the last act, the gamekeeper
comes upon the roguish poultry dealer (and sometime poacher)
Harašta, who boasts that he is marrying Terynka; the gamekeeper sets a trap for the Vixen, which she easily detects when
she approaches with her mate and their cubs; when Harašta re-
turns with a basketful of poultry, the Vixen feints lameness to
lure him into following her and to give her family a clear go at
the poultry; he stumbles, fires at random, and the exuberant
Vixen falls dead. Two epilogs follow this rousing scene: one outside the inn, where the gamekeeper boasts that he will soon get
the Vixen and is told that Harašta has already made her pelt into

Stanislav Lolek's drawing of the Vixen's courtship.

a muff for his bride, Terynka, at which the schoolmaster re-
signedly sheds a tear; and another in the forest (a reprise of the
first scene), in which the gamekeeper is again napping and
dreaming of all the forest creatures when he realizes the Vixen
is missing; startled into wakefulness, he catches sight of a fox
cub who is the spitting image of her mother the Vixen and vainly
lunges for it, only to find himself grasping the frog; but even this
frog is a grandchild of the one in the first scene, and the work
ends on a note of wonder and awe at nature's continuing renewal.

The opera was first performed on November 6, on a double
bill with Martinů's animal opera *Who Is the Most Powerful in
the World?* (Janáček's only comment on it was, "How come his

rooster has a better costume than *my* rooster?'') The year 1924 was an eventful one for Janáček and Brod both. Brod first saw the libretto early in 1923; his reaction was uncharacteristically reserved, perhaps because (as he said) he was unfamiliar with animals. He attended the Brno première and again saw the work when it was staged in Prague on 18 May 1925, but he did not get around to a translation before then. We shall pass over the intervening years for the moment to recount how this controversial translation came about.

In June 1925 Brod wrote Janáček that he had translated the first scene but foresaw many difficulties; he insisted that major changes were needed in the remainder if the work were to prevail on German stages and begged Janáček to give him a completely free hand. Brod regarded the Vixen as a symbol of youth, wildness, and nature; and he saw the three aging men as a trio whom life and love had quite passed by. Why not simplify matters for the listener and contrive it so that all three should have languished after the same girl, the ephemeral Terynka (who never appears in the opera); and why not turn her into a somewhat rowdy gypsy? And what about the final scene: was it meant to indicate the gamekeeper's impending death, as the Prague production had seemed to suggest? Kitsch! Brod would have the gamekeeper take solace in a vision of eternal love, and added the somewhat irrelevant point that he had depicted the opera's conclusion in that way in a book on Janáček that was about to appear—as if the composer were therefore somehow bound to accord post facto with his biographer's intent. Janáček was conciliatory at first.

JANÁČEK TO BROD, 16 JUNE 1925

The core of possible misunderstandings has been and remains the duo
Vixen Bystrouška—Terynka.
According to my notion, to which judging from your letter you also incline, the parallelism is between the *symbol* (Vixen Bystrouška) and *reality* (Terynka).
The symbol ends with the Vixen's death; reality doesn't get quite that far (Harašta marries Terynka); but even Terynka will

one day come to such an end! What else could one expect, since she's marrying such a vagabond (Harašta)!

This *prophecy* should be *expressed* by the gamekeeper! Perhaps at the place where he speaks to the schoolmaster of this "counterpoint."

Your concept when joined to these lines of mine will clarify all; no conjectures will be needed. Now be so kind as to work it out and the Czech text will be conformed in the new edition.

The piano score notes that the gamekeeper merely drops his gun in the last scene. Nothing more; let anyone make of it what he will.

What Mr. Pujman [the stage director of the Prague production, which bordered on the abstract] wanted to make of it—the gamekeeper in his death throes, etc., etc.—was dreadful.

The fox cubs and chickens must be sung by a children's chorus. That was another piece of Mr. Ostrčil's wilfulness, to unleash such monsters on the stage. [The conductor had tried to cast the shorter members of the regular chorus as the young animals, since no suitable children's ensemble was available.]

I am not likely to come to Prague just now. But I'd like to see your translation when it is finished. And here's to its completion. I am quite eager myself !

Brod took full advantage of this virtual carte blanche. Terynka became a gypsy child living at the gamekeeper's lodge who grows so unruly that her education is entrusted to the pastor, whom she brings into such disrepute that he is transferred—a closer parallel with the badger's rout in the first scene of Act II. That episode would no longer depend on the Vixen making water over the badger's lair, an impossible piece of stage business in Brod's view; instead, she would shame him by ostentatiously kissing him in front of everybody. Another impossible bit of staging, said Brod, was to end the opera with a reprise of the encounter between gamekeeper and frog; couldn't he say a few concluding words instead? (Brod might have done well to remember the two highly effective exits of the little blackamoor at the end of both the first and the last acts of *Der Rosenkavalier.*) Finally, Brod proposed that the crowd at the inn should abuse the parson in exactly the same terms in which the forest creatures abuse the badger in the preceding scene. This time Janáček was somewhat firmer.

JANÁČEK TO BROD, 26 JUNE 1925

1. It is impossible for Vixen-Bystrouška to kiss that badger! Motive for this scene: expropriative-communistic is the only one possible here!

2. And the end of the opera! Surely it is charming to let it end with the little frog! The music that goes with it is as if it were "tailor made." And the thing is original—and life's merry-go-round is thus truthfully and faithfully made plain!

Nor can any singing be inserted in the simple Coda (the music on the last page 182). Just ring down the curtain!

In his rapture the gamekeeper drops his gun—one milestone of life—and the little frog is a portent of his new consciousness.

I think your proposed concluding words, "So kehrt alles zurück, / alles in ewiger Jugendpracht" [Thus all comes round again, / Ever in glorious youth renewed], are already inherent in the scene.

3. On the other hand I fully agree with your suggestion *to repeat the second bar on p. 69* and to let the "populace" evoke the forest creatures (badger) in the enclosed motif: [two bars of music]. For the rest, I am glad that your "re-creation" is going well, too. But please, do oblige me in those two places.

Brod defended his adaptation by saying that he had not abolished the communistic expropriation idea at all but had on the contrary strengthened it by the additional agitation against the badger-faced parson, and again begged for a free hand with his difficult task of revising almost every word without changing the music. But Janáček remained obdurate with regard to the last scene.

JANÁČEK TO BROD, 3 JULY 1925

Liška Bystrouška was performed here [in Brno] yesterday.

The execution convinced me that they do fuller justice to it here than in Prague.

The final scene with the little frog—there's no help for it—it's charming! Let it be!

Have I told you that my *Šárka* and *Mister Brouček's Excursion to the Moon* are to be performed in Brno?

They played that piano piece for me yesterday. I shall let go of it.

The piano piece in question was what some critics regard as Janáček's most accomplished chamber-music work: his Concertino for piano and six-piece ensemble, to which we shall return. Meanwhile, Brod pressed on with the translation of the second and third acts. They were finished in July 1925, and his version was published as a separate German libretto. There were some compromises, yet Brod had his way in most instances. Above all, as for *Jenufa*, he was responsible for the title by which the opera came to be known abroad.

He had originally translated Liška Bystrouška as *Schlaue Füchsin* (Sly Vixen). In Czech, the word for fox is ordinarily female, *liška*; there is a derivative word for male fox, *lišák*—contrary to English or German, in which the male *fox* or *Fuchs* are the generic terms, and the derivative words for female fox, *vixen* or *Füchsin*, sound a little like diminutives. Moreover, *bystrouška* may be read as a diminutive noun derived from the feminine adjective *bystrá* (sharp, quick, acute)—just as *stará* ("old," a feminine adjective, but also a slang noun for "wife," like the German "die Alte," my old woman) gives rise to the more affectionate *starouška* (dear little old woman)—so that *bystrouška* could be "sharp little one" if the *ou* is pronounced as a diphthong in a three-syllable word, to rhyme with "THIS gauche car." That was doubtless how Brod arrived at his final title, *Das schlaue Füchslein* (sly little fox, since *Füchslein* is a neuter diminutive of both *Fuchs* and *Füchsin*). Brod's title was then rendered into English as *The Cunning Little Vixen*, which also reflects the traditional Aesopian view of the fox as a cunning animal. (Among words regarded as synonymous with *cunning* are *crafty, tricky, artful, sly, wily,* and indeed, *foxy.*) Yet recent years have seen attempts to render the title as *Vixen Sharp-Ears*, and to view Brod's title as spurious and imposed by a capricious Universal Edition in order to enforce its publisher's rights.

We do know that Těsnohlídek originally called the vixen *bystronožka*, which means "fleetfoot," since *nožka* is a diminutive of *noha*, "foot"; and that she became *bystrouška* through a misprint. But the diminutive for *ucho* (ear) is *ouško*, so that a word for "sharpears" analogous to *bystronožka* would have to be *bystro-ouška* (rhymes with "BIStro gauche car") or at most the noncompounded four-syllable *bystro-uška* (rhymes with "BIStro pushcart").

What all this etymological chitchat thus comes down to is how Janáček pronounced *bystrouška*: in three syllables or four. The word occurs eleven times in his score, the first time when the heroine introduces herself to her suitor-to-be. It is set to three notes every time, *by-strou-ška*. According to the composer's own intent, *Das schlaue Füchslein* (and *The Cunning Little Vixen*) is thus a more authentic translation than *Vixen Sharpears* (or *Fox Sharpears*). Brod was right about that, as he was about so many things. (Literary criticism is also returning to his views about Kafka, after a number of writers had declared them to be worthless.) And Universal Edition is quite right to insist on the more authentic title, which was after all sanctioned (in its German version) by Janáček.

We shall never know whether a version closer to Janáček's original would have assured the opera's success sooner than did Brod's "re-creation." We do know that Brod's version led to only one prewar German production, in Mainz in 1927, which closed after three performances. (One can only speculate on whether that was because of Brod's contributions or in spite of them.) A reorchestrated version introduced in Prague in 1937, under Václav Talich's direction and featuring the children's chorus of the broadcasting service, did not fare much better. Not until after the Second World War did the work gradually achieve international currency, most recently in something like the original version, which had been used in Czechoslovak opera houses all along. Czech musicians never thought much of Brod's improvements. Jaroslav Vogel, the same author who spoke so eloquently of Brod's acuteness and great skill in improving *Katya Kabanova,* took him severely and minutely to task for what he had done to the Vixen.

> The improvements suggested by Brod as such certainly sound very appealing and are certainly not devoid of ingenuity. Nevertheless, I cannot characterize them otherwise than as *one gross miscomprehension of the entire work,* and that mainly for the following reasons: (1) they wholly alter both the sense and

the fundamental character of the majority of the scenes, and (2) they thus break up the only right relationship between action and music. . . . All the objections I have voiced here are of course not to be taken as belittling in the slightest the truly great service that Brod did Janáček both by his enthusiastic and inspired articles and by his translations. Even in this case he acted only in an effort to serve the work; Janáček, who on the one hand—and certainly not without grounds—regarded him as a veritable oracle, and who on the other hand had not exactly had his self-confidence reinforced by the work's indifferent initial reception, understandably offered only mild resistance. (It is fortunate that among other things he insisted at least on the highly original ending with the pert little frog, which Brod had also denoted as "impossible.") Indeed, our master even expressed his willingness to make subsequent changes in the original to conform it to Brod's revisions. Yet it is significant that it never came to that; moreover, the last and probably decisive letter that Janáček wrote Brod in this whole affair has been lost.

Back to 1923.

In that year, Brod had largely completed the first biography of the composer, *Leoš Janáček: Leben und Werk,* which was immediately translated into Czech; in fact, the Czech version came out first, in time for the composer's seventieth birthday (on 3 July 1924), while Universal Edition was still making up its mind about the original. (Hertzka finally channeled the monograph to Wiener Philharmonischer Verlag in Vienna, which published it in 1925.)

Janáček was involved at this time in a petty, querulous, time-consuming correspondence with Kovařovic's widow, who continued to draw a one-percent royalty for the changes her husband had made in the *Jenufa* score. (During his lifetime, Kovařovic had quietly turned over his receipts from this source to his orchestra's welfare fund.) Janáček thought at first that these payments were deducted from his own royalties, or at least reduced the gross receipts on which his royalties were based, but even when he learned otherwise he continued to begrudge *any* payment to the heirs of Kovařovic, whose revisions he had resented in the first place. (Later he even threatened to withdraw all his works from the National Theater in Prague if the payments to

Kovařovic's estate did not cease, but Löwenbach talked him out of it.)

Although his creative powers were at their height, Janáček in his seventieth year could doubtless always hear time's wingèd chariot hurrying near. He naturally resented all calls on his time that took him away from composing. Even Brod's repeated entreaties for a more complete list of compositions were answered only in part, which led to some accusations of dilettantism when Brod's book appeared with an incomplete bibliography. (The most infuriating review came from the Brno musicologist Vladimír Helfert, at first a severe critic of Janáček but later an equally extravagant admirer, who undertook a biography of the composer so detailed and extensive that only a quarter of it was finished when Czechoslovakia was dismembered in 1939; the author died in 1945, before he could return to it, in part from the hardships he had undergone in a Nazi concentration camp.) Brod could find some consolation in Janáček's bland assurances that it was all his fault and that without Brod's book, Helfert would never have set out to prepare the more complete bibliography he published later that year. Besides, thanks in large part to Brod's efforts, Janáček was gradually becoming known abroad. Three events greatly advanced his fame during 1924: the spring festival of the International Society for Contemporary Music (ISCM), which took place in Prague (with a subsequent summer session in Venice), partly in honor of the centenary of Smetana's birth; and the Berlin and New York premières of *Jenufa*.

Janáček's debut before the mighty mandarins of modern music had taken place at the previous year's ISCM festival in Salzburg, with the first foreign performance of his Violin Sonata of 1914. The fine hand of Löwenbach had doubtless insured that Janáček would get his innings at last. The circumstances were enough to pique anyone's curiosity. Who was the white-haired gentleman with the funny name, born in the same decade as Elgar, Puccini, and Mahler (in fact, before all of them), who had forsaken the musical idiom of his coevals for that of composers thirty years his juniors, such as Stravinsky and Alban Berg? Like Berg, he was said to have written an important opera that practically no one had ever heard. (Apart from the wartime performances in Vienna and Cologne and two postwar performances in Yugoslavia, *Jenufa* had been staged only in Brno and Prague; and *Wozzeck* was not performed anywhere at all until its première in Berlin in 1925.) But that oversight at least was about to be corrected.

The long-planned Berlin première was announced for Sunday, 17 March 1924. Brod cautioned Janáček that it could be the making of him and begged him to take a leave from his various posts to spend a couple of weeks in Berlin. Let him participate in the rehearsals; let him call on Ambassador Tusar, who would arrange valuable introductions and other support. There would be no problem about the written materials that the Berlin State Opera's dramaturg, Julius Kapp, had requested for publicity—Brod had already dispatched a long essay on Janáček to Kapp for that purpose. That was easy for Brod: not only was he at work on the aforementioned Janáček biography, he had also published a collection of essays on the music and literature of Prague the previous year, *Sternenhimmel* (Starry Heavens), the first eight essays of which made up a monograph entitled *Zur Erkenntnis Leoš Janáčeks* (On Understanding Leoš Janáček). Its subject was so pleased with the result that he sent a copy of *Sternenhimmel* to Marie Jeritza, his erstwhile Vienna *Jenufa*, who had gone on to the Metropolitan Opera in New York. But he did not take Brod's advice to spend more time in Berlin. He would arrive Saturday afternoon, too late for the scheduled dress rehearsal; see the opera on Sunday; and depart on Monday. He would also find time to visit Frederick the Great's Sanssouci Palace at Potsdam, "to visit," as he wrote afterward, "the great *flautist,* to whose whistle the whole world once spun," and to have luncheon at the embassy. (It would be his only interview with Ambassador Tusar, who dropped dead of a heart attack five days later.)

One reason Janáček was not plagued by the sort of anxiety that had attended the Vienna première six years before was that the Berlin production was in the capable hands of one of the great conductors of the day, Erich Kleiber, who had once studied in Prague. On the contrary: at the extra dress rehearsal the management had thoughtfully added to fit in with Janáček's schedule, he was so undone by what he saw and heard—the huge orchestra, the well-prepared cast, the excellent staging—that he could not stop weeping and whispering to Kapp, "Dass ich *das* noch erleben durfte!" (That it was given to me to live to witness that!) Afterward, he wrote a glowing letter to the conductor.

JANÁČEK TO ERICH KLEIBER, 22 MARCH 1924

I am still thinking of you. You turned my work into a string of delightful sun-drenched peaks. The recruits' song and Jenufa's song had always come off as a hacking military march. You breathed the life of hot young hearts into it. "Every couple must live through its painful time of sorrow"—they made a sort of dirge out of it both in Prague and in Vienna. You gave it a smile. And that's how it should be. And all those dreadful *Luftpausen* [breathers] they would take in Act II. Your Act II achieved a classic plasticity. . . . Yours is the first well-conceived *Jenufa*, not the Prague nor the Vienna one! If I might ask anything at all of you it would be: (1) the introduction to Act I a little faster, to give it a suggestion of unrest. And put the xylophone on stage near that mill wheel. That will muffle its icy sound. That's all.

The Berlin *Jenufa* was a stunning success and as decisive as Brod had predicted. In rapid succession the work was accepted for performance in Munich, Karlsruhe, Kassel, Düsseldorf, Coblenz, Bremen, Hamburg, Breslau, Osnabrück, and Nuremberg. But even before the Berlin performance, Janáček received word that *Jenufa* had also been accepted by the Metropolitan. To the participants in the ISCM festival in Prague that spring, Janáček's name would not be quite as strange as it had been at Salzburg the previous summer. Besides, some inkling of his growing reputation had penetrated into the English-speaking and French-speaking worlds of music even before that.

The wave of interest in Slavonic culture that arose from the alliance between the Western powers and Tsarist Russia had broadened to encompass the newly liberated nations, especially Poland and Czechoslovakia. In Britain, Czechoslovakia had found a great champion in R. W. Seton-Watson, the founder of the *Slavonic Review* (now the *Slavonic and East European Review*). A British specialist in Russian music, Rosa Newmarch, became the great postwar champion of Czech and Slovak music. In 1922 she contributed an article on "Leoš Janáček and Mo-

ravian music drama" to the first volume of the *Slavonic Review,*
which ultimately led to an invitation to the composer to come to
Britain for performances of some of his works. The Swiss-born
music correspondent of *Mercure de France* and author of a book
on Smetana, William Ritter, wrote an article on Czech music
after Smetana (in which Janáček figured prominently) for Lionel
de la Laurencie's *Encyclopédie de la musique* in 1923. The
French writer and music historian Romain Rolland became fascinated with Czech music after hearing a private performance of
Smetana's 1876 string quartet "From My Life" during a visit to
Prague as President Masaryk's guest. And in America, Olin
Downes of *The New York Times* took a lively interest in the music
of Czechoslovakia, which he visited several times, the first time
for the ISCM festival.

Convening the festival in the Prague spring of 1924 was a
great feather in Löwenbach's cap, the successful achievement of
efforts that had extended over several years. He was madly busy
during the actual days of the festival (May 30–June 4) and for
some time after. To add to his chores at the festival, the ministry
of foreign affairs had asked him to look after some of the more
important visitors, notably Romain Rolland, whose official ci-
cerone Löwenbach became. And it was also Löwenbach who
arranged for Olin Downes to interview Janáček.

In a letter from New York written on the day of the Berlin
Jenufa première, the stage director of the Vienna première, Wymetal, had confirmed that the Metropolitan Opera had definitely
scheduled a New York performance for the 1924–25 season.

WYMETAL TO JANÁČEK, 17 MARCH 1924

Having just heard that the Metropolitan and Universal Edition have concluded an agreement and that a performance of
your *Jenufa* in the course of the coming season here is now assured, I hasten to express my great pleasure and to send you my
heartiest congratulations! I think I can say in all modesty that I
did my stalwart bit in bringing it about, since Director Gatti
very rarely mounts an opera he does not know; moreover, it
meant carrying the day against the formidable competition of a
warmly and authoritatively recommended production of *The
Flying Dutchman,* with Mme. Jeritza as Senta. But now *Jenufa*

is victorious and I look forward to what will certainly be a splendid rendering of the work. Besides Mme. Jeritza in the title role and Mme. Matzenauer as Kostelnička, other major singers are also being assigned to all the remaining parts. The presence of Maestro Bodanzky at the podium guarantees flawless musicianship, and for the rest it goes without saying that I shall give my all toward a successful production.

In addition to directing, Wymetal had been charged with commissioning the sets and costumes, and had asked for picture postcards of men, women, and children of all classes in Moravian costumes to be sent to his address in Vienna, to which he was returning the following month. The costumes would be made in Czechoslovakia, so that they would be "even more elaborate and characteristic" than those for the wartime Vienna première six years before.

Once the proposed production became general knowledge in New York's musical circles, Olin Downes decided that he must try to meet Janáček during a forthcoming trip to Europe. On

Stage design for the Metropolitan Opera's 1924 American première of *Jenufa,* Act I.

the advice of knowledgeable friends he wrote Löwenbach to en-
list his aid. Downes's first plan was to see Janáček in Prague,
but the composer demurred and asked Brod to substitute for
him.

JANÁČEK TO BROD, 11 JUNE 1924

A reporter from some New York paper or other has arrived.
He has come specifically to see me. He was in a wreck on the
flight from London to Prague. Now he is in Prague.

Today I had a call from *Lidové noviny*; I am supposed to
come to Prague for the interview.

I can't do that.

Please do ask Dr. Löwenbach about this American reporter
and come to an arrangement with him. You know what to tell
him better than I do.

He is supposed to speak only English.

Brod, half out of his mind with grief—it was the week of
Kafka's funeral—nevertheless replied civilly that he could not
meet any American journalist just then and that such a meeting
would be bound to be unsatisfactory in any case, since he spoke
no English. Downes had meanwhile concluded that having come
this far he might as well travel the remaining 200-odd kilometers
to Brno to visit Janáček, which he did early on Saturday evening,
June 14, with an interpreter.

The resulting article occupied almost a full page in *The New
York Times* for Sunday, 13 July 1924. It was devoted mostly to
Janáček but also to a few other Czech composers, especially
Alois Hába, who had devised a piano with a quarter-tone scale
and was developing a new theory of harmony for it. The description in the interview proper is worth quoting in full, since it is
the only contemporary account of Janáček and of his views as
seen through American eyes.

Janacek is now 70 years old [wrote Olin Downes, who was
then 37], white haired, but singularly vigorous, not at all the
type of a starving and uncomprehended dreamer, but a very full-
blooded personality whose dominant tone is that of a fresh ide-
alism and a great pleasure in living. A visit paid him in his little

home in Brunn was interesting for many reasons. He lives in a house built for him in the garden of the Brunn Conservatory, where he teaches a few hours of each day, devoting most of his time to walks in the country and composition. He waited long for success, which did not come to him in any considerable degree until "Jenufa," composed and first performed in Brunn twenty years ago, was given in Prague in 1916 and thereafter in a number of European cities. His happiness in his present circumstances and his success is naive and without any pretense. Correspondents run out to see him, there is a succession of visitors of high and low degree, and Janacek is frequently taking the train to Vienna or Prague or Berlin to hear his operas performed. He told a friend recently that he would take every opportunity of enjoying his music that he could since he had not many more years to live and had gone without such experiences for so long. While we talked the composer pulled out his notebook—page after page scribbled with hasty notations. "Sparrows," he said with a laugh, and, turning the page, "trees, * * * bells." On another page: "Songs of peacocks and other birds, of which we had recently an exhibition." Again, "A sausage seller at the railroad station," and "A child in its little carriage; and"—he scribbled lustily—"it is you as you say, 'Yes; yes.'" There it was on paper. Janacek repeated emphatically that he never used these motives in their literal form, and he never used popular melodies. "That," he said, "would only be repeating the words of some one else." He talked in Czech rapidly and evidently with such a wealth of native metaphor that even a devoted disciple well acquainted with English found it difficult to translate for him.

"And what composers," he was asked, "have influenced you most?"

He answered, succinctly: "None."

"Well, then, what composers do you admire most?"

"Chopin and Dvorak."

"Dvorak more than Smetana?"

"For me—yes."

"And what operas do you prefer?"

He had heard Moussorgsky's "Boris Godunoff" for the first time a year ago and admired it very much. This opera and Charpentier's "Louise." But he was tiring of "Louise."

"And Wagner?"

"No. It is not only that he is too symphonic, and that the

orchestra usurps the stage, but that his system of motives is at once too detailed and too inelastic. The same motive invariably accompanies the same character, and, although it is frequently transformed, it has not sufficient resource and flexibility within itself to reveal the constantly changing emotions and motives of the character that the composer attempts to portray."

"Do you like 'Pelléas et Mélisande'?"

"To a certain point, but there is too little melos. It is too much speech and too little song. Melody cannot be replaced in music, and I prefer a better balance of symphonic style and musical diction than Debussy believed in. In certain places in my operas the orchestra takes a musical phrase from the singer and expands it. The phrase is absolutely truthful, and the instruments, in such instances, carry out its implications as no human voice could. Opera must be an organic whole, based equally upon truthful declamation and upon the song which the composer must evolve from his own creative spirit."

Of "Jenufa" there will be more to say when it is given in New York next season. Whether the theories and the dramatic style of Janacek will make as strong an impression in America as they have in his own country and in parts of Austria and Germany is to be seen. His opera, with Mme. Jeritza in the title rôle, will have scenery prepared under the direction of Czech artists, and costumes which are now being made by the peasant women of Moravia, whose exquisite designs and needlework it would take a page to describe. Music of Janacek which shows a composer of very true and strong dramatic power is his chorus, "The Seventy Thousand," sung with unforgettable effect by the Prague Teachers' Choir. This chorus expresses the anguish of 70,000 Czech miners who found themselves for a period under the domination of Germany on the one side and Poland on the other, in Silesia. The[y] cry: "We are seventy thousand! You have ready for us seventy thousand graves, but we will live!" It is a superb composition, and as sung by the splendid amateur choir of school teachers, which Method Dolezil directs with enthusiasm and mastery, made an overwhelming effect. Certain passages were as the voices not of some forty singers but of thousands prophesying war. As the climax approaches there are cross-rhythms, and an inspired use of the highest and hardest registers of the tenors—an effect of intense and incoherent excitement. "We will live! We will live!" That cry had a force,

suddenness and certainty as if it had been flung, with one ex-
plosion of feeling, on paper.

Jenufa was not a success at its New York première on
6 December 1924, possibly because it suffered from some of the
same drawbacks that had marred the Vienna production. Wymetal's overly literal and almost corny staging overwhelmed the
piece; and the statuesque Marie Jeritza, got up in a richly em-
broidered gown that is still a Met showpiece and that made her
look at least eight feet tall, overwhelmed the rest of the cast. As
bad luck would have it, the influential English music critic Ernest
Newman, who was then working as a reviewer in New York, took
a dislike to the piece and panned it mercilessly. "A more complete collection of undesirables and incredibles has never before
appeared in opera," he wrote in the *Evening Post*. Olin Downes
was more generous and factual (though he did manage to mis-
spell Brod's name), but Lawrence Gilman was scornful. "There
is nothing very seriously the matter with 'Jenufa' except the music," Gilman wrote in the *Herald Tribune,* and went on to point
out the obvious parallels with Musorgsky. "But Janacek lacks
what Moussorgsky had so abundantly—the power of musical invention. Janacek's music has all the preliminaries and accesso-
ries: honesty, feeling, psychological insight, theatrical skill; it
lacks the one essential . . . the ability to write music that in
itself, as a pattern of tones, is eloquent, expressive, memora-
ble. . . . Hearing it once, one has no wish to hear it again."

The unfavorable reviews were to kill *Jenufa* in New York for
half a century. It was not performed again at the Met until the
1974–75 season, five years after the more adventurous San Francisco Opera first offered it in 1969. Janáček would probably
never have learned of the impression his masterpiece made in
America—certainly not from the enthusiastic report he was sent
from New York by the star of the show.

JERITZA TO JANÁČEK, 20 JANUARY 1925

Many thanks for your nice note, which gave me great pleasure. A thousand pities you couldn't be here with us for your
Jenufa. It would have given you great pleasure. And it really

was a wonderful performance. Once again, congratulations from the bottom of my heart. I can imagine what great joy the news that *Jenufa* is to be revived in Vienna as well must have given you. Hope to see you again on that occasion.

However, the Prague music journal *Dalibor,* stronghold of the Smetana forces, gleefully reprinted excerpts from the New York reviews, a clear case of *Schadenfreude*; so Janáček was not spared yet another humiliation at the hands of his detractors.

One aspect of the New York production (which the Met also took to Philadelphia) did give Janáček pause: his royalties. When he received the derisory sum of $100, he wrote Marie Jeritza for information. She wrote back that the payment was an improbably low one and did not tally with the Met's usual rates. Nothing in the Janáček archive shows that the sum was ever augmented, but a search of the Metropolitan Opera's archives yields a copy of the contract the company concluded with Universal Edition's agent, the Berlin theatrical agency of Norbert Salter, on 18 March 1924. Under this contract, the Met was to pay $250 for each performance, half for the composer and half for the publisher (the publisher's half to include the hire of the parts and, presumably, the agent's fee). A check for $1500 for the six performances went off on 7 April 1924—a young fortune in the inflation-ridden Berlin of the day. Janáček's share should have been $750; if he really got only $100, he had good grounds for complaint. If he did not pursue the matter, it was because he had meanwhile become deeply involved in another major operatic project, and in the festivities by which his native land recognized his achievements at last.

Janáček's seventieth birthday on 3 July 1924 initiated a year of performances of his music throughout Czechoslovakia. What made it extraordinary was that they included several world premières, since he was then at the very peak of his creative powers. *Jenufa* was produced in Prague on the great day itself, but not by the National Theater, which could not bestir itself to take part in the celebrations; it was the provincial Brno company that offered the work in Prague, at another theater. In July 1924 he completed the wind sextet *Youth,* a lively piece whose third movement contains a trio that had started out as a merry march for piccolo, glockenspiel, and small snare drum dedicated to the Bluebirds, his youthful fellow scholars at the Brno Queen's Monastery. Turning seventy might easily set anyone to reminiscing, but the ever forward-looking Janáček was not the man to immerse himself in nostalgic regrets. Still, he may have felt importuned to take a backward look. Brod had been pressing him for details for the biography he was just completing; so had a Brno journalist, Adolf Veselý, who was putting together a memorial volume for the occasion. In addition, 1924 was not only Janáček's year but Smetana's—the centenary of his birth—and Janáček might well have been mindful of his illustrious predecessor's famed autobiographical quartet "From My Life," which had so impressed Romain Rolland when he had heard it in Prague that spring. And what a pretty how-d'ye-do that had turned into! Rolland had declared that he was less and less interested in the past and more and more in the present, in which he detected a new vigor and—in the case of Czech music—a new sensibility. He must have also said something about Smetana, which was reported by Paul Neubauer in the *Prager Tagblatt* to the effect that Smetana was a good musician, with his heart for music in the right place, but of diminishing interest just then because in Rolland's view, all that needed to be done would be done by the newer Czech music—a damning by faint praise that he partly disavowed in a subsequent interview. Yet someone who had evidently overheard Rolland's remark (and who had perhaps misinterpreted his French) compounded the confusion by reporting it to Janáček as a preference for his music over Smetana's, a judgment with which Janáček would have had no difficulty at all. When Brod's biography came out that summer in Czech translation and the Czech press was slow to take notice of it (except for Helfert's aforementioned nitpicking review, which had so incensed Brod), biographer complained to biographee and received a consoling reply.

JANÁČEK TO BROD, 14 AUGUST 1924

Have no fear; they'll write about your book, all of them. But now, my friend, it's vacation time! If it were someone else's star besides mine it would wake them from their slumber. But the reason for such meanness is that all this business with me and you coincided with the Smetana year. Then only one constellation was meant to shine:

Nejedlý—Smetana.

If only those Prague hacks could have heard Rolland's judgment about Smetana and about me! There were witnesses there enough.

I really stay at home all the time; I am done with a suite "Youth" for wind instruments (fl., oboe, clar., French horn, bassoon, and bass clarinet).

It's finished—and I leave content for Luhačovice tomorrow.

Janáček's scathing and spontaneous mention of Zdeněk Nejedlý, a musicologist and publicist who was to become Communist Czechoslovakia's first minister for cultural affairs, is especially interesting because Czech musicologists have been at pains to play down his opposition to Janáček's music, some going so far as to claim that Janáček had been prejudiced against Nejedlý by none other than Brod, who detested him. It is next to impossible at this remove to sort out all the esthetic, national, and above all political passions that might have played a part in any subsequent recounting of these relationships, especially in a society in which the depth of one's respective allegiance to the music of Smetana, Dvořák, or Janáček might well translate directly into eligibility for jobs, honors, and all sorts of other perks. (Even personal relationships may have played a part: Nejedlý was said to have favored Smetana over Dvořák because he had once proposed to Dvořák's daughter and had been turned down.) It is also true that Brod remained Nejedlý's implacable detractor to the end, decades after it could have been of any consequence.

In his 1960 biography Brod wrote of Janáček:

> Even after the success of *Jenufa* he continued to be knocked about by many Czech critics, especially those under the influence of the highly esteemed university professor and musicologist Nejedlý. From what I can gather about present-day Czech music life, Professor Nejedlý (now minister of culture) has

changed his stand on Janáček. Doubtless because folklore has now come up trumps. While Janáček was alive, Nejedlý attacked him precisely for folkloristic tendencies. How times change!— One of Nejedlý's students regularly sat beside me at openings. We were both music critics and to some extent shackled together as colleagues. Incidentally, nearly all the important music critics of the day were Nejedlý's students. His antagonism toward Janáček dominated public opinion.—It was just after I had begun to voice my enthusiasm for Janáček's music abroad. I kept it up. Every time I entered the theater, my beloved colleague greeted me with the following phrase, in Czech: "Listen, Brod, you've got yourself out on a fine limb with that Janáček!" For a young man like me it wasn't easy to withstand the repeated onslaught of these suggestively hurled words.—I like to tell this story to spur on young people today to resist and persevere against all sorts of twaddle in the arts, no matter how authoritatively stated.

Another instance of ex post facto deference to the party line is an editorial comment on Janáček's casual remark that his music was rooted in real life, a statement that was later used by musical ideologues eager to inveigh against "Western formalism." (Such people were ever more comfortable with Smetana's programmatic music than with the more abstract music of Dvořák, just as Soviet musicology reflected the all-important fact that Stalin's favorite composer was Tchaikovsky, while the greatest Russian composer of the twentieth century, Dmitry Shostakovich, floated in and out of official favor according to how closely he hewed to "socialist realism.") On 2 August 1924 Janáček wrote Brod derisively about musicologist Josef Hutter: "A man who went on and on in my presence how only a pure tonal line had any meaning in music. And I say it means nothing if it is not rooted in life, in blood, in the milieu. Else it is a toy we need not value." To which the editor of the Janáček–Brod correspondence appends dutifully, "One of Janáček's most beautiful pronouncements about the ideological, programmatic, and realistic nature of his music, which sweepingly contravenes all suppositions about his formalistic tendencies." During the 1950s the pressures for conformity became even greater. The writer Milan Kundera (then still in Prague) reported how he had actually heard a sycophantic candidate for a degree in film parrot

the official line about Janáček: "formalist . . . naturalist . . . estranged from the people and from the present." Writing in the
magazine *Nový život* (Modern Life) in 1954 Kundera took to task
the toadies who would measure Janáček's achievement by a
"home-made ruler of a Marxist esthetic." Actually, argued Kundera, Janáček's music reflected the plight of a pure, ostracized,
sensitive individual ground down by an inhumane society—the
drama of a richly human man in conflict with a callous environment.

Youth received a less than professional first performance at
the Brno Conservatory on 21 October 1924, during which the
malfunctioning of one of the clarinet's keys came close to turning
the sextet into a quintet. (The proper première took place a
month later in Prague; this time *seven* members of the Czech
Philharmonic did the honors, with an extra flutist playing the
piccolo.) The Brno performance was part of a celebration that
also included a Sunday morning concert of Janáček's choral
works and (on 6 November 1924) the world première of *The
Cunning Little Vixen*—music enough to exhaust the concertgoing
public of even the proudest of small towns: a fourth event, which
was to feature works from Janáček's early period, had to be
canceled for lack of interest. (Brno is the size of Rochester, N.Y.,
another conservatory town, which might also be hard put to provide audiences for four closely spaced performances devoted entirely to the works of a local composer—say, Howard Hanson.)

Brod had gone to Rome in mid-September on a government
grant to do research and soak up background for his historical
novel *Rëubeni*. He was back a month later but begged off coming
to the Brno festivities so that he might write down his Italian
impressions while they were fresh. He would come to the Prague
concerts (he wrote Janáček on a postcard) and hoped to sight
the *Vixen* when the National Theater offered it, which would
surely be before long. Janáček wouldn't hear of it and professed
to believe that it was mainly Brod's newspaper job that was keeping him back.

JANÁČEK TO BROD, 31 OCTOBER 1924

How could you possibly miss *The Cunning Little Vixen* in
Brno!

Painting by Czech cartoonist Dr. Desiderius (Hugo Boettinger), now in Jarmil Burghauser's possession. Nejedlý had described Dvořák as "a boulder that every Czech composer had to clear away before he could go on." The painting shows Nejedlý as "Sir Zdeněk to his armor bearers: 'You're to roll this *boulder* [capped by Dvořák's likeness] out of my way; it's of no further interest to me!' " To the right of Nejedlý are composer Otakar Zich and musicologist Vladimír Helfert (marked by a baron's coronet, since his family had been ennobled).

Dr. Brod has attended me for a lifetime, and when I want him to stop over for my best work—is he to be absent?

First of all, it's no good writing right after gathering strong impressions—Italy, etc. When another stratum of life has settled on top of these impressions, invention wells up the more richly for it—and more torrentially. An artesian spring.

Second: you won't hear the *Vixen* in Prague too soon and not like here. Members of this cast are as if molded for each part.

Third: I should like to know why Dr. Brod couldn't serve
the *Pr. Tagblatt* even while he is on the train, or while he spends
those few hours in Brno. Must he stick to that editorial den,
then? What you'll see and write—it will be worth it.

I am writing this after a rehearsal in which I heard the entire
Vixen.

I think I have convinced you and will see you here at noon
on November 6.

Brod did attend (and review) the performance, which was
just as well, since the opera did not reach Prague until the following May. Meanwhile Prague had heard the Brno *Jenufa* and
the première of Janáček's First Quartet, which he had completed
in 1923, a splendid work that is in the repertory of string quartets
the world over to this day. He dedicated it to the Bohemian
Quartet, which first performed it at an evening devoted to Janáček's chamber works put on by the Society for Modern Music at
the 400-seat Mozarteum recital hall on 17 October 1924; the
composer Josef Suk (the quartet's second violin) did some arranging of the parts. A repeat performance took place three days
later in the much larger Smetana Hall, not quite as effective.
And that was not the end of the Prague festivities, which continued with the aforementioned performance of the seven-man
sextet, another performance of it at an all-Janáček piano and
chamber-music recital at the Prague Conservatory five days later,
and an all-Janáček concert of choral and orchestral works, with
the Czech Philharmonic directed by Václav Talich, on 8 December 1924. That was a gala occasion and a highly emotional experience for Janáček. President T. G. Masaryk attended and
honored the composer by inviting him to the presidential box,
and the usually stolid and sophisticated symphony subscribers
gave the composer ovation after ovation. Janáček was in seventh
heaven. "I felt, you know, a sort of wave coming at me," he said
afterwards. Nor was that all. The following month the Masaryk
University of Brno voted an honorary doctorate for Janáček,
whose academic qualifications until then began and ended with
the teacher's credentials he had earned at a normal school.
Deeply gratified, he never failed to put "Dr ph." before his signature for the rest of his life.

It is not given to many composers to celebrate their seventieth year by presenting the world with three new works of the caliber of *Youth,* the First Quartet, and *The Cunning Little Vixen.* The quartet has remained the most often performed of the three works—perhaps of all his works. It is subtitled "Motivated by L. N. Tolstoy's *Kreutzer Sonata"* (which Tolstoy wrote under the influence of Beethoven's famous sonata for violin and piano), a somber novella about love and adultery and a woman's self-fulfillment, a theme that had occupied Janáček since before *Katya Kabanova* and to which he was to return with a vengeance in his next major work.

Throughout his year of honors, in fact as far back as the end of 1922, Janáček was thinking about basing an opera on a play by Karel Čapek, Czechoslovakia's foremost playwright and novelist. In a letter dated 22 August 1922, Janáček inquired of Brod: "Do you know Čapek? RUR, The Insect Play. His sister said something about a libretto." Čapek had become world famous with his play *R.U.R.* (Rossum's Universal Robots, the title that had introduced the new word *robot* into English, derived from the Czech *robota,* forced labor), in which machines take over the world and acquire human feelings, including love. In 1922 he had another hit, *Věc Makropulos* (literally, the Makropulos case, although "secret" would be nearer; it is rendered in German as *Die Sache Makropulos* and in English as *The Makropulos Affair),* on an equally fantastic theme: a beautiful woman who survives for over three centuries, only to come to long for death. Janáček saw the play in Prague in December 1922 and wrote Čapek early in 1923 to inquire about the possibility of basing an opera on it. The letter has not been preserved—Čapek later gave it to a collector and it has disappeared—but his reply alluded to a previous discussion.

Čapek to Janáček, 27 February 1923

> As I told you previously, I have too high an opinion of music—especially yours—to be able to imagine it connected with such a *conversational,* most unpoetic, and overly wordy play as

my *Makropulos Affair.* I fear you have something different and better in mind than my piece—apart from the 300-year-old figure—really affords.

But no need to take these my sincere doubts into consideration; what is worse—as I learned on inquiring of my agent František Khol—is that I am bound in this regard by a contract with the American (and world) agent H. Bartsch, to whom I had to guarantee, in accordance with current usage, that the work would be neither filmed nor set to music for 10 years. I don't think it would be feasible to get out of that clause of the contract.

On the other hand, my dear Master, there is nothing to prevent you from inventing, quite separate from my play, a plot in which living and enduring a span of 300 years would be the axis and focus in a setting more suitable than my piece affords. After all, it's not my patent; you could choose for example Ahasver, the woman magician in Langer's story (in his collection *Assassins and Dreamers*), or for all I know Miss Makropulos, and rearrange the plot to suit your requirements entirely independently, in whatever way—insofar as you told me of your inspiration—you see this material. Surely you can't use the long discussion of a lawsuit, of a lost recipe and its utilization, etc. In all these regards my text would have to be altered so extensively that it would be doubtless more advantageous not to follow it at all but to create one's own circumstances.

I repeat that I do not regard the fiction of an eternal or three-centuries-old person as my literary property and that nothing stands in the way of your using this fiction in your own manner.

Čapek was being excessively nonchalant in describing the plot of his play as a standard one. Could he have had misigivings about a musical setting of his play? Perhaps he suspected that the piece might become better known as Janáček's opera than as his play (which is in fact what happened), much as Ferenc Molnár is said to have refused the use of his 1909 hit *Liliom* as a libretto for Puccini—only to have it become even more famous as Rodgers and Hammerstein's musical comedy *Carousel*. It is true that the story of Ahasuerus (not Esther's biblical king Xerxes, but the Wandering Jew) had been knocking about European literature for a good deal longer than three centuries. It had fascinated Czech writers, including perhaps Čapek's contemporary František Langer, ever since the Eternal Jew, as he is known outside France and Britain, had been reportedly sighted in Prague in 1602. (The related story of Faust was likewise claimed as a Czech legend, by the historical novelist Alois Jirásek.) The idea has captivated such diverse writers as Shelley (*Queen Mab,* 1810), Eugène Sue (*Le Juif errant,* 1844), Hans Christian Andersen ("Angel of Doubt," 1848), and James Hilton (*Lost Horizon,* 1933). Čapek might have also mentioned Bernard Shaw's 1921 play *Back to Methuselah,* except that he was still unaware of it. But it was precisely Miss Makropulos that Janáček wanted and none other: once again, Goethe's elusive *Ewig-Weibliche,* another idealization of Janáček's beloved Kamila Stössl, to whom he was to write, "Come and see that 'woman grown frigid,' *you'll see your own portrait,*" and again, "*You're* poor Elina Makropulos."

Janáček's libretto for *The Makropulos Affair* begins with an exposition of a century-old lawsuit over the estate of a Baron Josef Prus who died in 1827 without issue and without leaving a will. A relative's claim to the estate was contested by Prus's ward Ferdinand Gregor on the grounds that he had been once introduced by Prus as his prospective heir; the relative contended that it was not Ferdinand but one Mach Gregor who was so meant and who never turned up. The suit is still before the courts as the play opens, at the turn of the twentieth century. When the lawyer of Ferdinand Gregor's grandson Albert Gregor recounts the story to the famous opera singer Emilia Marty, she mysteriously asserts that Ferdinand Gregor was actually the baron's son by the singer Elian MacGregor, so that he was the unknown "Mach" Gregor; and that a will in his favor may be found in a sealed yellow envelope in the Prus house. It is found and does designate the testator's illegitimate son Ferdinand as the heir, but Emilia Marty refuses all rewards; she is only interested in finding still another envelope, one containing a Greek manuscript, which she believes must be in the same house. Challenged to offer proof that the said Ferdinand is identical with Elian MacGregor's son, she promises to produce one. But her opponent, a descendant of the Prus family, learns that the birth register shows the son's name as Ferdinand Makropulos, not Gregor. Emilia Marty insists she can clear that up as well, but first Prus must find and sell her the Greek manuscript; she asks him to name his own price. He proposes a night with her, to which she cooly assents; and so she gets the manuscript at last. (In a series of subplots, she is depicted as icy cold to all men, including Prus's only son Janek, who shoots himself when he learns that his chief rival is his own father.) The proof of identity she now produces is an evident fake—although backdated a century, it is in her handwriting—and a search of her luggage yields letters addressed to various women's names, all beginning with E. M. The denouement is at hand: she explains that she was born in Crete in 1575, the daughter of a Dr. Makropulos who became the court physician to the emperor Rudolf II and provided him with a recipe for an elixir that would allow him to remain young for three hundred years. The emperor ordered it to be tried on the physician's daughter first and, when she lost consciousness for several weeks, jailed her father as an impostor. But she got better, escaped with the recipe, and has lived until the present under various names—Elina Makropulos, Ekaterina Mishkina, Else Müller, Eugenia Montéz, Elian MacGregor, Emilia Marty. She lent the recipe to her lover Baron Prus and has been frantic to recover it because she is now three hundred and thirty-seven years old and is beginning to age. But now she has it she realizes she no longer wants it—and neither does anyone else. An aspiring young singer (the dead Janek's fiancée) takes it from her and burns it—and Elina Makropulos falls dead.

Čapek's nonchalant letter did not exactly amount to a formal permission to proceed; Janáček would not be caught out again as he had been in 1887, when he had finished most of *Šárka* to Zeyer's libretto without his permission, only to have it denied at last. But in September he got a more definite commitment.

ČAPEK TO JANÁČEK, 10 SEPTEMBER 1923

Forgive me for delaying my answer to your letter regarding *The Makropulos Affair* for so long. I was waiting for my representative, who was traveling, and without whom I did not want to undertake anything.

I now incline to the view that the American agent (and owner of the world rights) can make no objection to a Czech-language musical setting. You are thus free to set my piece to music and since I am simply never going to get around to any sort of re-writing or arranging, I am giving you the right to rearrange my text in accordance with your needs.

I should have liked to give you something better to set to music than this piece of all things; but if you feel drawn to it, you will surely make something great of it, and I most fervently and with all my heart wish you the best of luck.

Janáček started on the opera right away. Within a couple of months, just before Christmas, he was able to report good prog-ress to Brod.

JANÁČEK TO BROD, DECEMBER 1923

I have done over 200 pages of *The Makropulos Affair*; it's truly an unfettered flight, you know. Full of themes, I shan't see how to make them come together until the end of Act I. But I will go to the Tatra mountains for the holidays. That white, silent snow cover as far as the eye can see forces one to settle down and think.

Despite the good start, *The Makropulos Affair* was not fin-ished until 12 November 1925, in part because Janáček repeat-edly set it aside to turn to other works: the First Quartet, *Youth,* and his Concertino, which he wrote in April 1925. In May he was in Prague for the ISCM festival, during which *The Cunning Little Vixen* was first performed in Prague; in September, as a conciliatory gesture toward his wife, he took her along to Venice for the second half of the festival, during which his First Quartet received its first performance abroad. This time he had to com-pete with the works of such well-known European composers as Fauré, Hindemith, Honegger, Ibert, Malipiero, Ravel, Roussel, Schönberg, Stravinsky, Szymanowski, and Vaughan Williams. He also suffered a tragicomical indignity. Wearing a white sum-mer suit, he left the auditorium to make his way to the stage of the Teatro Fenice for a bow after his quartet, only to find himself in the street. He was rescued at last and taken backstage through a dusty underground passage, arriving somewhat disheveled and a bit the worse for wear; however, the applause was still continuing, and he was recalled several times.

Another interruption came when *Šárka* was performed in Brno at last, and Janáček participated in preparing the production, as he wrote Brod.

JANÁČEK TO BROD, 25 OCTOBER 1925

Thank you for your novel and my book [Brod's *Rëubeni* and his Janáček biography in the German original].

I have started reading the novel.

But right after coming back from Venice I became painfully ill; I've been clenching my teeth for three weeks now.

I got *Šárka* ready for the Brno performance and wanted to leave for Hukvaldy.

Ah well, it can wait a week.

They're already copying Act II of *The Makropulos Affair.*

But now I feel like a run-down horse who's being fed on straw instead of oats.

Nothing tastes good to me, either.

Schönberg etc. etc.—all the world wants to write *merry music*—but it all misses the point.

The last sentiment derived from the impressions Janáček had gathered in Venice and had echoed in a newspaper article published in *Lidové noviny* on 8 November 1925:

Believe me, if you don't know it, that music by itself cannot proclaim love nor hate nor sadness nor joy. It knows how to laugh, but that laugh won't evoke a laugh. It contains neither jest nor irony nor satire nor humor nor joviality nor burlesque nor persiflage nor travesty nor masquerade.—And there is such a demand now for merry music. . . . And all Schönberg takes hold of in his Serenade op. 24 is the Viennese twang of a mandolin or guitar.

The *Makropulos Affair* was not to have its première until the end of 1926, but by then Brod had already negotiated a contract with Universal Edition and was hard at work on a translation, which he made from the printer's proofs. In little over a week

Act I was done and on its way to Vienna; on 22 October 1926 he reported that he had begun a new novel, *Die Frau, nach der man sich sehnt* (The Woman One Yearns for). But a few days later he began to run into trouble with the translation, of the same sort he had experienced before: lack of continuity, insufficient motivation for the chief character's actions, wrong accentuation of foreign words. Two main bones of contention emerged: a reference to the unopened envelope with the recipe for the elixir of life, which the unwary listener might confound with the envelope containing the will; and Brod's change near the end by which this second envelope would be taken from Emilia Marty, then returned to her, and then taken away once more. Janáček would have none of Brod's attempts to avoid the confusion and strengthen the plot.

JANÁČEK TO BROD, 9 NOVEMBER 1926

> I can't get it out of my mind!
> If they were to take the envelope, give it back to her, and then take it from her again, Marty would scratch all their eyes out like a wildcat!
> I should have to reflect that action in the music and I'm not going to.
> It would be a mere theatrical gesture—and it's unnecessary.
> I should be reproached for a big gap at that point. I beg you to leave out the corresponding theatrical remarks.
> I am writing [Universal] *Edition* that I am asking you to leave all that out.
> I don't know where these passages are, so please write Edition, too.
> Let Marty clasp the hardwon manuscript triumphantly to her heart—and then decisively cast it away.
> As the manuscript burns to an ash her death approaches apace; no need to involve it in unnecessary stage business!
> I'm sure you'll agree.

That was all very well, replied Brod respectfully, but the two envelopes were still too easily confounded; Marty was no wildcat at that point—in fact, she had fainted; and the ending was much too abrupt, since her motivation for giving up the manuscript after all she had done to regain it was by no means clear. In short, Brod thought the work would never hold the stage if these incongruities remained. However, there *was* a way out: let the Czech text hew to Janáček's original but let Brod's alterations remain in his German translation, which would be revised so that no further changes in the music would be needed. Janáček agreed to that but made a stand on the one point that had bothered him most.

JANÁČEK TO BROD, 11 NOVEMBER 1926

As to the further explanation why Marty does not want the envelope after all—*I agree with that.*

With your phrase [in a conformed Czech version] "I have felt death near and thought it not so frightful"—*I even agree with that.*

But to take the envelope from her and then give it back—I can't go along with these theatrical gestures because they're not in the music. That I, whose music bows down when a zephyr ruffles the grass, should now omit to capture a *new* musical theme when they tear the manuscript on which her life depends out of the monstrous Marty's hands!

That would be a grievous error. Keep all you propose, only do away with those two gestures!

I don't know why I am so afraid *for myself* here.

The last sentence reflects the tristesse that sometimes overtook Janáček toward the end of his life. And even the cited phrase about death was already a compromise: a similar wording had been previously rejected in a discussion that Brod recalled in an obituary the day after Janáček's death. "Impossible," Janáček had said, "I can't compose to that. Death—and not frightful?" His niece Věra also remarked in a letter of 1940 on how much her uncle had hated the very idea of death:

It was not fear, it was a strong determination to avoid, as long as possible, not only death itself but all reminders of it. He never went to funerals or cemeteries, he wanted to hear nothing of the dead and only rarely spoke of them. In the old days he would visit churches for atmosphere, preferably Emaus [the church of a former cloister that for a time housed the Prague Conservatory]. But in later years I could not get him into a church even to shelter from the rain. 'A church,' he told me, 'is concentrated death. Graves below the flagstones, bones at the altars, pictures all about martyrdom and dying. Pews, prayers, hymns, death and death again. I don't want to have anything to do with all that. [When his mother died, he had suddenly become too ill to attend her funeral.]

As always, he soon bounced back. Things were finally going his way. There was growing recognition abroad and a substantial income at last. Brod attended the Brno première of *The Makropulos Affair* on 19 December 1926; so did the critic Paul Stefan. Both reviewed it at once. (It was not performed in Prague until 1 March 1928.) Brod published a review in the *Prager Tagblatt,* which Janáček disliked but acknowledged. "But!" he wrote Brod on 28 December 1926. "That review of *The Makropulos Affair* was not written by the old Dr. Brod." A few days later he took up the struggle with Brod over changes introduced in the translation once more. Secure in his success, Janáček was more than ever inclined to stick up for himself.

JANÁČEK TO BROD, 2 JANUARY 1927

I have had it drawn to my attention by several people that the translation of Act III of *The Makropulos Affair* is too free.

I started reading it and enclose the instances that could be corrected, at least in the separate libretto. [There follow no fewer than fifty-two bracketed bilingual passages, of which six are underlined in red as particularly objectionable; in a fifty-third passage, the composer reverts once more to the phrase on which he had previously compromised:]

P. 181/5 [In Czech:]   I have felt death near, felt its hand reach for me.
                         And it wasn't quite so frightful.

        [In German:]   Wonderful how death's touch could be tender, gentle.
                         And that had filled me with such dread?

And I would stick with the original:

[In Czech:]   Sorry I had to be gone a short instant.
                   Blinding headaches, sharp relentless
                     pain
                   For the past two centuries.

There is to be no sentimentality here.
What next? Too late to make corrections in the piano score.
But the separate libretto remains to be printed; they could still go into that.
I have reproached you for everything. Most notable are the deviations underlined in red. Your translation was too free in those instances, it lacked that hardness of the original.

Janáček's letter hit Brod very hard, coming as it did on top of the reproach about his reviews of the new opera, which he had thought had been warm and enthusiastic. It looked as if he was in for a replay of the prolonged struggle over the translation of *The Cunning Little Vixen*, only this time with Janáček taking a much firmer line. He was practically accusing his translator of being a traitor, as in the Italian epigram, *traduttore—traditore*. Patiently, Brod replied that he was somewhat surprised to see Janáček reopening questions that had long been settled—hadn't Brod agreed to the one restoration on which Janáček had insisted (the business with the envelope), and weren't all the other changes intended merely to clarify the one point that wanted clarification, which was why Emilia Marty would suddenly give up the recipe after moving heaven and earth to gain it? But all right: Brod would make some further restorations, his only wish was to keep Janáček satisfied. Still, this was no mere translation: the byline on the title page would read, "Translated and edited for the German stage by Max Brod."

Anyone who has ever translated anything imperfect (such as a composer's own libretto) must sympathize with Brod in this interchange, which dragged on for another month. How his fingers must have itched to make the requisite improvements! He was an experienced writer—a published poet, novelist, and playwright—whereas Janáček's deficiencies in stagecraft were only too apparent. On the other hand, Brod revered Janáček's genius as a composer and had been among the first to recognize it; when it was a question of which came first, words or music, nothing less than strict adherence to another well-known Italian aphorism would do: *prima la musica e poi le parole.* The two strong-minded men had reached an impasse. But at that point the mercurial Janáček suddenly backed off and ended by accepting most of Brod's changes, in a more conciliatory letter dated 9 January 1927. Yet he couldn't resist adding at the end, "Well, I thank you for the review, but it didn't set the world on fire! It didn't set Berlin on fire!"

In that he was quickly proved wrong. Within a month Berlin had accepted *The Makropulos Affair,* and Janáček, perhaps partly in expiation, wrote a characteristically impressionistic, enigmatic, moody open letter to Brod that appeared as a feuilleton in *Lidové noviny* on 13 February 1927 under the title "What I Believe in."

> I too sought the flow's source with a divining rod; but for a wonder, wheresoever I found myself, near a mountain, near a bog, before the wind, in the lee: the rod dipped down everywhere! At least the dew shone on everything toward which my rod inclined. Even in a desert there was a freshening.
>
> In the telephone receiver, in the dust of centuries-old manuscripts; in the flag where it fluttered above the Castle in the mad March days: yes everywhere there sounded a note in a theme that was oppressive in tears, piercing in vengeance, belligerent, rent in anger, splintered in quarrel.
>
> It is night. A clang in my apartment's pipes. I stiffen: am I to be inundated? Current penetrates metal in a rush. [Sketch of a musical chord repeated thrice.] And as the water spreads, it smacks and licks the funnel. [An arpeggiated flourish, also thrice.] It flows and overflows!——
>
> In a like way, were I to think in terms of composing, I should get right down to the *truth,* down to the rough speech of the elements, and I should know how to progress through art.
>
> On that journey I do not tarry with Beethoven, nor Debussy, nor A. Dvořák, nor B. Smetana; for I do not meet them along the way. I do not borrow from them, since I can no longer pay them back.
>
> Here I approach F. M. Dostoyevsky. I found in *The House of the Dead* a good human soul both in Baklushin and in Petrov, as well as in Isaiah Fomich.
>
> [In Russian:] *Molodets'* [fine fellow] Isaiah Fomich!

You were the first, Dr. Brod, to see that depth of expression. But enough of that.

Abel's sacrifice comes to mind. The fire blazes up in a straight flame and loses itself in a plume of smoke. So fervent were your words about *Jenufa.*

The gnats and the wasps and the beetles had their wings and shells burnt off! I was able to finish *The Makropulos Affair.*

We might both now stop and think. I feel as if the pen were about to drop from my hand. Out of breath, at a loss—I wait to see whether some little star from the distant sky might yet descend to ring the changes of my mind.

I am at ease. I breathe as nature breathes in the spring sun. Everywhere green promise, here and there a curious blossom. I would perceive nothing less than the wingbeat of the music of the spheres.

. . . .

Perhaps it is at an end, the exhausting effort of persuasion, Dr. Brod?

. . . . .

Tame as a dog, fierce as a vulture, dry as a wilted leaf, smacking of life as the crashing waves, sputtering like brushwood being consumed by fire. Receptive to every stirring of the mind—and silenced in the holy stillness.—

It is time now to speak of Janáček's life and other works during the prolonged travail on *The Makropulos Affair*—prolonged in part because it did not occupy him exclusively. There are hints of two of the works in the open letter to Brod: *Naše vlajka* (Our Flag), a short *pièce d'occasion* for two solo tenors and *a cappella* male chorus, which he completed early in 1926; and *From the House of the Dead,* which was to become his last opera. But there were three other major works as well, his Concertino, Sinfonietta, and the *Glagolitic Mass*; and two lesser ones, *Capriccio* and *Nursery Rhymes.*

Janáček completed the Concertino in rustic Hukvaldy in April 1925; it was first performed on 16 February 1926 in Brno and four days later in Prague by a young woman pianist, Ilona Kurzová-Štěpánová, who later gave a highly successful performance of it at the 1927 ISCM festival in Frankfurt. (The work is dedicated to Jan Heřman, a pianist whom Janáček greatly admired.) Janáček wrote numerous pieces for piano, at least three of which remain in the repertory of the shrinking ranks of recital pianists: *On the Overgrown Path,* fifteen short pieces he wrote between 1901 and 1908; the cycle *In the Mists,* which he wrote in 1912; and the two-movement sonata *1. X. 1905,* written in memory of František Pavlík, a young workman who was bayonetted to death on that date when soldiers of the Austro-Hungarian garrison broke up a Czech protest meeting in Brno. (Janáček burnt the third movement and later threw the other two into the river Vltava during a visit to Prague, where, according to his own account, the manuscript pages "floated on the surface like white swans" and refused to sink; luckily, the pianist, Ludmila Tučková, had secretly made a copy of the two movements, which is all that remains.) But the four-movement Concertino is the nearest thing Janáček wrote to a composition for instrumental soloist and orchestra. It is in fact a virtual piano concerto and is sometimes directed by a conductor, even though the accompanying ensemble comprises only six instruments (two violins, viola, clarinet, French horn, and bassoon) and in each of the first two movements the piano is supported by a single wind instrument (horn, clarinet); the full ensemble does not enter until the end of the second movement. The piece thus builds in intensity from beginning to end, especially in the piano part, which goes from a simple melodic line in the first movement to more elaborate chords in the second, octave passages and a proper cadenza in the third, and thundering chords and octave runs in both hands in the fourth movement, ending in a highly effective stretta. Yet this is no academic piano concerto but a lively, programmatic piece that Janáček originally thought of as a suite to be called "Spring," in which the first three movements were to represent various animals and the last a cascading river. The work is thus a recital-hall counterpart of *The Cunning Little Vixen* (which also first took shape at Hukvaldy), much as the Russian literary context of the First Quartet recalls *Katya Kabanova.*

The five-movement Sinfonietta, really a short symphony consisting of the regulation four movements and an introductory fanfare that is recapitulated at the end, was written in a matter of three weeks in March 1926. The work started as another *pièce d'occasion,* fanfares for the nationwide quadrennial jamboree of the patriotic and gymnastic Sokol (Falcon) Society that was to be held in Prague the following summer. Janáček later designated the movements as Fanfares, The Castle, Royal Monastery, A Street, and Town Hall—all references to his beloved Brno. The city's name goes back to the Celts who inhabited Moravia during the pre-Christian era and derives from the Celtic *brynn* (meaning "hill," as in Brynmawr, the Great Hill, the Welsh district after which the Pennsylvania village and college are named). There are actually two hills: one above the old town (which contains the town hall and the monastery where Janáček had lived as a schoolboy); the other, Spielberg, crowned by an ancient castle-fortress. "The flag where it fluttered above the Castle" in the open letter to Brod, which one might assume to mean Hradčany castle in Prague, may just as well have referred to this fortress, which had been a murderous political prison in Austrian days. But now Czechoslovakia was free, with its own citizen army, and the fortress had become one of that army's barracks: what a transformation! The deeply patriotic Janáček referred to the work as his "Military Sinfonietta," a tribute to his faith in the reborn nation. It was first performed during the Sokol *slet* (gathering of the Falcons) by the Czech Philharmonic under Václav Talich on 26 June 1926, an occasion for which Janáček skipped that year's ISCM festival in Zurich.

The *Glagolitic Mass* had its origins in an unlikely encounter, five years before, between the anticlerical Janáček and Leopold Prečan, the Archbishop of Olomouc (Olmütz), whose official summer residence was at Hukvaldy. (On a previous occasion, when invited to an archiepiscopal audience, Janáček had sent word that he was too busy. "Let him come to me," he had added irreverently. "He's the archbishop of the Catholics, and I'm the archbishop of the musicians.") The two had fallen into step during a ramble through the woods, and Janáček (who actually liked the archbishop quite well personally and was to dedicate the completed work to him) had casually mentioned the weak showing of contemporary church music. The prelate had challenged him to do something about it. Janáček did give it some thought afterward but balked at using a Latin text. Not until 1926 could he lay his hands on an annotated text in Old Church Slavonic, the language dating back to St. Cyril, the Greek missionary to the Moravians, who with his brother St. Methodius had brought Christianity to the Slavs in the ninth century. (The title of the work is a bit peculiar: *Glagolitic* refers to the alphabet, not the language.) This work was begun during an August holiday in Luhačovice and was completed on 15 October 1926. It was first performed on 5 December 1927, in Brno. The mass itself followed the Latin version almost verbatim, although that signified no return to the faith of his ancestors for Janáček, who remained a determined agnostic. Janáček's pupil Ludvík Kundera (the father of the present-day emigré novelist Milan Kundera), a pianist and musicologist who was charged with preparing the piano score for Universal Edition, incautiously suggested in writing that "the oldster Janáček, a firm believer," must have felt ever more urgently the absence from his oeuvre of an element that would express his relationship to God, and received a terse postcard from the master for his pains: "No oldster, no believer!" Like the anticlerical Verdi in his Requiem, Janáček gave an almost unseemly operatic character to the sacred text; indeed, he appeared to think of it in operatic terms, if we interpret his directions in the piano score—that a passage for three offstage clarinets during the orchestral interlude following the Credo should be played *za scénou*—literally as "behind the scene," a locution more closely associated with the theater than the concert hall. At any rate, the work leaves a most powerful impression on the listener, not least because the customary postlude (an organ solo) is followed by a triumphant orchestral passage that seems to affirm a lust for life not generally associated with the genre.

Janáček was at the pinnacle of his fame during the years following his seventieth birthday. In October 1925 Brod, returning from a trip to Paris, reported that Henry Prunières, publisher of *La Revue musicale,* wanted to devote a whole issue to Janáček, and that the Paris music dealer Jan Sliwinsky (who had introduced Brod to Prunières) would mount a display of all Janáček's works in his shop if at least one copy of each were sent him. (It was done, but the sales were disappointing.) In 1926 *Jenufa* was performed in German both in Prague (under Alexander von

Zemlinsky's direction) and in Brno, as well as by almost every German opera company of note; it had previously been done in Yugoslavia and was now produced in three Polish cities as well—altogether in about seventy European opera houses that year. Bruno Walter was inquiring about *Katya Kabanova* for the Berlin City Opera. Only *The Cunning Little Vixen* failed to get a run. (It finally received its German première in Mainz on 13 February 1927, yet to Brod's puzzlement was not taken up anywhere else.) But the most gratifying event of all was an invitation to visit Britain from Rosa Newmarch, acting as member of an official committee that also included the conductors Adrian Boult and Sir Henry Wood, the composer Ralph Vaughan Williams, and the principals of both the Royal Academy of Music and the Royal College of Music.

Not since Dvořák's visit forty years before had any Czech musician received the full force of the sort of treatment that only the British establishment knows how to accord distinguished guests. He was wined and dined, driven in Sir Henry Wood's car to his country house, given receptions at Claridge's and the Czechoslovak Club, invited to submit his biographical data to *Who's Who,* and generally handed the keys to the city. Ambassador Jan Masaryk (son of Czechoslovakia's president and himself a highly talented amateur pianist) personally looked after him and took him to see Seton-Watson, the doyen of Britain's Slavonic scholars. But the high point of the visit, an all-Janáček concert in Wigmore Hall, almost did not come off. Britain's great General Strike of 1926 had just started, and there was no way to publicize the concert and no way for the public—or the performers—to get to the hall except on foot. (It took Leon Goossens, then the oboist of the London Wind Quintet, three hours to make it.) Nevertheless, the evening was quite well attended. Each work and the names of the players were announced by the manager—there were no printed programs—and enthusiastically received: the First Quartet (played by the Woodhouse Quartet), the Violin Sonata, the sextet *Youth* (played by the London Wind Quintet with bass clarinetist Haydn Draper), and the *Fairy Tale* for cello and piano. (The Concertino, originally scheduled to cap the evening, unfortunately had to be canceled because pianist Fanny Davies, a student of Clara Schumann's, kept playing it too romantically, and a frantic telegram summoning Ilona Kurzová-Štěpánová from Prague was returned because it had been inadequately addressed.) The strike also meant no reviews, so that the actual purpose of familiarizing the British public with a new star on the musical horizon was served only partially. (*Jenufa* was not to be staged in London until 1956.) But Janáček was overwhelmed by the respect being paid him— that would show them at home!—and rushed from event to event, tiring himself out so much that he was glad of a respite in Holland when it turned out that he had arrived there two days before the date of his sleeping-car reservations.

Back in Brno, more good news: Bruno Walter's inquiries about *Katya Kabanova* for the Berlin City Opera had borne fruit, and the work would be performed on 31 May 1926. Otto Klemperer had mounted an earlier German production in Cologne in 1922, but this was Berlin, whose 1924 production of *Jenufa* had launched that work on its international career. To be sure, that had been at the State Opera under Erich Kleiber, whereas *Katya Kabanova* was to be done at the City Opera under Fritz Zweig. But not to worry! Brod had heard from the prima donna of the German opera house in Prague, Tilly de Garmo (who would be going to the Berlin State Opera the following autumn) that Zweig was doing a bang-up job of the new production—and she ought to know, since she was Zweig's wife! (Zweig also transferred to the State Opera the following year but returned to his native Bohemia after the Nazi takeover and spent the next five years at the German opera house in Prague with George Szell and Max Rudolf; all three had permanently left Czechoslovakia by 1938.)

At Brod's suggestion, Janáček traveled to Berlin (with his wife) for *Katya Kabanova* and once more came away full of enthusiasm.

JANÁČEK TO BROD, 10 JUNE 1926

> At last I can be myself again in a quiet corner. I should have liked to have seen you in Berlin. Maestro Zweig prepared the work beautifully and directed it excellently.

But the reviewers tear into the City Opera on principle! We were as if ground between the upper and nether millstones!

And still it was a splendid performance, the like of which we can't even dream of in Prague and in Brno!

Both the State and the City Opera asked me for *The Makropulos Affair*. The translation (into German) is ready, it only wants submitting.

Those London string and wind players have hearts of ice! They are content with half measures. They sit in front of their fireplaces—and can't stand the heat of the sun!

My *Military Sinfonietta* is to be played in Prague (the Philharmonic) on June 26. But I don't know whether it will come off. Mr. Talich sits in Stockholm and will soon be standing in Zurich—and the orchestra is left in the lurch in Prague!

Schrecker and Schönberg came to me with compliments about *Katya Kabanova*! That pleased me best of all.

Strong perceptions strongly felt; and further evidence that Janáček had gained assurance and sophistication enough from his successes to comment on such worldly topics as the rival factions siding with one or the other of Berlin's public opera houses, the degree to which the strikebound islanders in London managed to involve themselves in his music, the persistent problem of the internationally known resident conductor who is perceived as neglecting his orchestra whenever he undertakes a guest engagement elsewhere, the fact that both the impressionist Franz Schreker and the twelve-tone pioneer Arnold Schönberg had gone out of their way to praise his work (as did Marie Jeritza, who was in the audience), and above all the growing conviction that domestic productions of his operas paled next to those in foreign capitals—a point to which he reverted again and again. In a feuilleton written shortly after his return from Berlin, Janáček set down his impressions of the production while they were fresh: "And how the storm storms in Act III, in an orchestra of 95 players! Such performances dazzle. They fling the door wide open to send the work on its way in the world." And the following year, in reply to a poll conducted by the German-language daily *Prager Presse* on the question What are you giving for Christmas?, Janáček wrote testily, "I only wish it would cease to be a legend that our theaters—large and small—are a component of the Czech cultural enterprise. They are nothing of the sort, not by half."

On top of all this activity, Janáček also managed to complete two less extensive but by no means minor works, Capriccio and *Nursery Rhymes.* Several piano compositions for left hand alone had been written for Paul Wittgenstein, who had lost his right arm in the First World War: the well-known concerto by Ravel, another by Prokofiev, and two pieces by Richard Strauss. The Czech pianist Otakar Hollmann had been similarly wounded, and Janáček undertook to write a four-movement piece for the left hand for him, accompanied by a flute and six brass instruments, which was completed on 11 November 1926. (It was first performed in Prague, by Hollmann with members of the Czech Philharmonic, on 2 March 1928; Janáček attended.) The Capriccio is subtitled "Defiance," which has been variously interpreted as a tribute to the maimed pianist's determination to pursue a virtuoso career, the composer's undying opposition to war and all its horrors, and his willingness to defy all the world in his love for Kamila Stössl, who is represented by the uncommonly stately and joyous flute part.

Nursery Rhymes was, like *The Cunning Little Vixen,* based on excerpts from the children's supplement of Janáček's favorite daily, *Lidové noviny.* The rhymes were short verses accompanied by the drawings of various artists, of whom the most prominent was Josef Lada, now known the world over for his comic illustrations of Jaroslav Hašek's *Good Soldier Schwejk.* Janáček's version started out as eight pieces for three women's voices, clarinet, and piano, and was actually performed in that version on 26 October 1925. But on his return from that year's ISCM festival in Venice, he began to have misgivings about humor in contemporary music, which he voiced in the previously cited feuilleton of 8 November 1925. In part to show what he was driving at, he rescored *Nursery Rhymes* for nine voices and an instrumental ensemble of ten, and enlarged it to eighteen pieces and an introduction. The new format was one that had challenged composers from Haydn to Stravinsky. In conscious emulation of Haydn's *Toy* Symphony, the scoring provided for an ocarina and a toy drum, but no part of the work was written to be performed by children, although it was intended for young

Illustration for Říkadla (Nursery Rhymes) by Josef Lada, the *Good Soldier Schwejk* illustrator.

audiences. Janáček wanted the published version (which Universal Edition was to publish in Brod's translation) to include the original illustrations. Always ahead of his time, he even suggested that they might be projected on a screen, in color, just before the start of each rhyme—an idea that may yet be taken up in these multimedia days, much as the lighting effects suggested by Alexander Skryabin have been realized in the psychedelic enhancement of his tone poems and as indoor "pops" performances of Tchaikovsky's *1812* overture substitute laser lights for fireworks.

There is a gap in the correspondence between Brod and Janáček from February to November 1927. Only a few postcards and short notes have been preserved. It is unlikely that there were no letters at all, but there could not have been many, since both men were deeply preoccupied. In the first proper letter, which Brod wrote on 9 November 1927, he confirmed that he had completed the revision of his translation of *Nursery Rhymes* for Universal Edition, but that he could do no more for the moment. We may wonder why he picked this particular assignment over all the rest, given the press of other work. There is a possible explanation. In the autobiographical novella *Beinahe ein Vorzugsschüler* (Almost an Honor Student) that Brod wrote in his seventies, he proudly cites his first attempt at rendering the rolicking rhyme and rhythm of Čelakovský's classic Czech ballad *Toman and the Woodnymph* in German, extra work he did as a teenager for a favorite teacher.

Do Podhájí k myslivci	Nach Podháj ins Jägerhaus
Musím ke své děvčici;	Muss zu meinem Lieb hinaus.
Z nenadání—nemám stání,	Bin im Bangen—wie gefangen—,
Zas mne čekej o svítání.	Will im Frührot heimgelangen.

(To my lassie's I must ride,
She's the Podháj huntsman's child;
Wherefore borrow pain and sorrow?
Look you for me on the morrow.)

If his keen pleasure in this teenage effort persisted for threescore years, one can see why he could not pass up the double challenge of translating popular verse *and* fitting it to a master composer's music. For the rest, Janáček would simply have to wait; although Brod had declared his willingness in principle to translate the resuscitated *Šárka,* he wouldn't get to it for several months at least (he never did get around to it), and his doctor had prescribed a rest after fifteen months of uninterrupted work. But it had been worth it: the first press run (15,000 copies) of his new novel *Die Frau, nach der man sich sehnt* had sold out in six weeks, and the book was being reprinted. Brod had also been working with Hans Reimann on the German dramatization of Hašek's *Good Soldier Schwejk* for Erwin Piscator, which was to be put on in Berlin early in the New Year and would launch that work on *its* international career.

Another pause in the correspondence ensued. Janáček was hard at work on his last opera. Finally, during the Christmas vacation, he broke his silence.

Janáček to Brod, 27 December 1927

Where have you got to?
Not a sound, not a trace of you? In good health? In Prague?
You don't even know that I have written
 A Glagolitic Mass
and that it is much revered?
The Frenchman William Ritter writes about it with enthusiasm. It is being published by Edition.
A happy New Year to you. I'll be in Prague on 7 January 1928; perhaps I can reach you.

Brod replied at once that he was looking forward to the visit, that the success of his novel was continuing (it had now sold 35,000 copies), and that he was glad to learn about the success of the *Glagolitic Mass,* which had received its world première in Brno on 5 December 1927. William Ritter had been there and had been quite bowled over; on his way back, he wrote Janáček a gushing letter from Strasbourg, in French.

Ritter to Janáček, 17 December 1927

It is with a very great sadness that I found myself in Prague *morally* unable to retrace my steps to return to Brno,—despite your so very friendly invitation and my desire to accept,—to hear another performance of that astonishing *Glagolitic Mass,* a work I truly hope will turn out to be another triumph for you. When I left you it was my intention to come back. But alas! I left behind—in addition to an altogether magnificent *chef d'œuvre*—a fresh tomb . . . and each turn of the road that took me away from it rent my heart a little more. My arrival in Prague signified the end of a great effort, which I felt I could not duplicate all over again. I know myself: once back in Brno, I must needs resume the road to Myjava [in Slovakia]. And the call of the *Glagolitic Mass* would have in turn summoned up that corner of a foreign field where henceforth will lie the remains of him whom I had most loved in the world. . . . It was to *conquer* myself that I had to forgo the music, marvellous and fiery as it is, born under those beautiful white locks of yours.

Ah! *Maître,* you are fortunate . . . ! With each passing day and each new work you grow more worthy of love and admiration. You don't know how that Mass did upset me! Now I'm going to transcribe some notes that I so greatly regret not having completed on that great structure that reminded me so much of the wooden church of Kecsmarok [a seventeenth-century Slovak landmark], a very cathedral among structures of that sort, and that gave me the courage to call you *Podkarpatsky Michelangelino.* . . . And that diminutive *ino,* "a little Ruthenian Michelangelo," should delude you neither as to the nature nor as to the degree of my admiration. It does not confer a second rank, it does not classify, it means simply "a sort of Michelangelo" on the scale of which the architecture and the art of the dear little wooden churches admits. It is clear that in that art your work has done its best. And from now on one could say about it that, in this art, the only actual cathedral is better than the great Protestant church of Kecsmarok, it is a musical cathedral.

Despite all I subsequently heard in Prague, my brain never ceased to be galvanized by the vestiges, the traces left in it by that first hearing and to restore for me the ineffable total emotion under the shock of the abrupt appearance (after the preliminary orchestral rehearsals) of the work in its entirety at last, with all its choirs and its voices. I am most anxious for the score to be published so that I may more readily find the most emotion-filled pages. A more complete study is to come; meanwhile, a first article will describe the unexpectedness of that first revelation, and that as soon as I get back to Bissone [his residence in the Italian part of Switzerland, on Lake Lugano].

Au revoir, cher Maître. Thank you for giving me a little of your most precious time. I shall be back in Czechoslovakia this summer and hope very much to see you in Brno once more, or in the country.

The editor of the Janáček–Brod correspondence, to which the above letter is appended, chastely omits to identify Ritter's deceased friend, but it was obviously his beloved long-time collaborator, secretary, and translator Janek Cádra, a native of

Myjava and Ritter's constant companion since 1904, when Cádra
was twenty-one. (Ritter had also befriended another young man,
Josef Červ, whom he met in Prague in 1922 and later adopted;
he is known as Josef Ritter-Tscherf and still lives near Bissone,
in an old-age home in Morcote.)

The letter is further evidence of the international renown Janáček had begun to acquire in his lifetime. The *Glagolitic Mass*
had been ready for a year before its first performance at the end
of 1927—an eventful year that had also seen a first performance
of the Sinfonietta (under Otto Klemperer) in New York and
Berlin; Janáček's election, with Schönberg and Hindemith, to
the Prussian Academy of the Arts; a first performance of *Jenufa*
in Antwerp, which earned Janáček a Belgian decoration, the
Order of King Leopold; and first performances of the Concertino
in Dresden and during the ISCM festival in Frankfurt. (The festival was accompanied by an exhibition on Music in the Life of
Nations, to which Janáček had persuaded the government to send
the village band of Myjava; it proved to be a great hit.)

During a visit to Prague early in the new year, Janáček called
on Brod, found the apartment deserted, and wrote him a note
before returning to Brno.

JANÁČEK TO BROD, 10 JANUARY 1928

Today, January 10, I called on you at 4 p.m. I knocked and
knocked; to no avail.

I wanted to see you about the translations
1. of *Šárka* and
2. of the *Glagolitic Mass*.

Well, and about various other things. The *Glagolitic* and *Šárka*,
both will be easy. But it is urgent. The *Glagolitic* is to be published by the end of March and *Šárka* right after that.

I was invited to come to Leipzig for *Jenufa*. But I'm not
myself after the grippe. I didn't go.

I am finished with Dostoyevsky's *From the House of the
Dead*. The score is already being copied.

It is the first time,—that I don't know what to do next. But
I am glad of it. I am off to Hukvaldy for a couple of weeks; I
need the rest.

This year has been like a soul in fire.

I'll be back within three weeks; we'll set a meeting time.

Brod was back three days later—he had been in Berlin to help with Piscator's production of *Good Soldier Schwejk* (the cartoonist Georg Grosz was doing the stage designs) and urged Janáček to come earlier, if possible for the 21 January 1928 performance of *Katya Kabanova* at the German theater in Prague; the conductor was a twenty-eight-year-old newcomer, George Szell's predecessor Hans Wilhelm Steinberg, who Brod thought was a budding genius. (Later, as William Steinberg, he was to take the Pittsburgh Orchestra to major-league status.) For the rest, Brod suggested, perhaps it would be better if the Mass and *Šárka* were translated by someone else—he was completely exhausted—and he would get to *From the House of the Dead* later, since that was not quite as urgent. (That is in fact how events ordered themselves.)

Janáček did attend Steinberg's *Jenufa* première with Brod—and brought Kamila Stössl, whom Brod met for the first time on that occasion—but before that he wrote a highly personal letter to Brod, agonizing over his continuing passion for Kamila and enclosing a self-searching piece called "The Gathering Gloom," which he had written for a popular magazine.

JANÁČEK TO BROD, 18 JANUARY 1928

Have a look at the enclosed feuilleton. The editors of *Venkov* (The Countryside) had asked me for a few words.

You know my themes grow from the earth, animals, people—in all, they fasten onto anything *that is*. Anything but *klaviatura* [that is, the element of synthetic artificiality that a keyboard interposes].

The personification of my characters in the operas always wants really to live.

My Katya etc. is not a mere musical invention.

Tell me, might one disclose who the personification of my themes is? Has any writer done it? Painters can make no secret of it. Any composer? Would it be taken amiss if this spiritual relationship, this artistic relationship were to be exposed to the public?

She approves, since she and I regard ourselves as absolved of the indictment of any liaison except a purely spiritual one.

As you see from the article, this spiritual relationship has lasted 13 years and has never exceeded those bounds, even though it is based on friendship. That is incredible, but that's how it is.

Can anyone hinder it? e.g., can a wife hinder it?

I am aware of the psychological aspect of this propensity of the theme to lean toward actual impressions. The perception of the theme is accelerated and gains assurance, freshening.

That's evident in my works!

In this way I have grown and matured as a composer.

We'll see each other on January 21. Give me a friendly answer to my queries.

It is dreadful for mundane thoughts to rake one till they would draw blood.

This is without doubt the most intimate letter Brod ever received from Janáček, who could never bring himself to take the decisive step, very likely because of the scandal that leaving his wife for a young Jewish matron would have caused. (To Kamila he wrote in frustration: "I feel I must find a way to state openly what you are to me. I can't even wait for Brod. I'll tell it in a way that anyone will find convincing. You shall be raised up, elevated above all calumny.") He had turned to Brod, thirty years his junior, because Brod was vastly more experienced, a man of the world and writer on erotic themes who had coined a well-known aphorism that went to the heart of this very situation: "Friendship with a woman—it is not an idiom. It is an inexact description that omits what is most essential and emphasizes the inessential." Now, in the last year of his life, Janáček was indirectly charging Brod—as Kafka had done—to set it all to rights ultimately. And in his autobiography Brod did cite a revealing passage from a letter that Janáček had written Kamila a few months earlier.

JANÁČEK TO KAMILA STÖSSL, 8 AUGUST 1927

In my compositions, where we are stirred by pure feeling, sincerity, ardent truth, there are you: you're the source of the most tender melodies, you're that gipsy girl with a child in *The Diary of a Vanished Man,* you're poor Elina Makropulos, and you're the lovable youngster Alyey in the *House of the Dead.* If the

ribbon that binds me to you should ever break, my life's thread
would snap with it.

Brod also described an incident, a vignette that he had directly from Kamila's husband, who had witnessed it.

> Janáček was friendly with Frau Kamila Stössl toward the end
> of his life; he was often asked to dinner at her house. But al-
> though he had otherwise grown used to a lifestyle of middle-
> class comforts (though not luxury) in his later years, he loved
> to eat in the kitchen. I think that youthful memories, maternal
> ties, echoes of the modest village environment may all have
> played a part there. An eyewitness, the aforementioned Frau
> Stössl's husband, conveyed the following little scene to me,
> which went back to the time when Janáček was working on his
> *House of the Dead.* He couldn't find the theme for one of his
> main characters, a much-tormented young woman. Suddenly a
> fiery light from the kitchen stove fell on Frau Kamila. Janáček
> stared at her. "Now I've got it"—and at once, in the middle of
> the meal, he began to jot down his wild hooks of notes on paper.

By "one of his main characters" Brod doubtless meant Akulina,
who never actually appears on stage but is vividly described by
one of the prisoners as he tells his story; the only female part in
the opera is "an ugly wench" (prostitute) who has exactly three
lines.

Apart from the few exceptions cited previously, few of the
seven hundred letters Janáček wrote Kamila have been made
available for publication to date, although most are in the Brno
archive. But Janáček also left behind a musical equivalent, his
Second Quartet, which is a final paean to his love and admiration
for Kamila. During three weeks after his return from Prague,
he laid everything aside to compose this minor masterpiece. His
original intent was to make the viola d'amore one of the instruments, to call the work *Amorous Letters,* and to have it first
performed by a professional quartet in Písek, where the love of
his life continued to reside sedately with her husband. (It was
also the residence of the famous violin pedagogue Otakar Ševčík, whose students, led by an enterprising American violinist
named Lipkin, had formed a quartet and had already performed
Janáček's First Quartet; and of Cyril Vymetal, a professor at the

national school of forestry there, a composer's son, amateur conductor, and a great organizer of musical events, who by his own
account had made Písek, "from 1924 to 1928, perhaps the only
Bohemian provincial town in which Janáček was regularly and
successfully performed.") None of these intentions was realized.
The work was scored for a standard string quartet. It was called
Listy důvěrné—literally "Leaves in Confidence," but usually
rendered in English as "Intimate Letters." And the first public
performance was a posthumous one, in Brno, by the Moravian
Quartet, on 11 September 1928. Not that Janáček had given up
easily. To the last he tried to coax his champion Cyril Vymetal
into a Písek première.

JANÁČEK TO CYRIL VYMETAL, 27 JUNE 1928

They played my second quartet, *Intimate Letters,* for me today.
The Moravian Quartet played it brilliantly. Their fee should be
augmented by the third-class round-trip fare betwen Brno and
Písek.

It's a trip that would take them two days.

I would not want to have the whole evening given over to
my works alone. That would be an inadmissible imposition, un-
forgivable.

How do you propose to cover your expenses?

You could vary the program by having young Firkušný play.
He could play after the Dvořák quartet; and again, with
Mr. Kudláček [the leader of the Moravian Quartet and another
Ševčík pupil], my Violin Sonata; and then could come the Second Quartet. I realize you want Firkušný for a separate concert
with the [Písek] orchestra. However, an evening of chamber music would serve to introduce him and, most important, the sonata
would need no rehearsal. I could have a word with Firkušný and
see to his fee.

I'll ask Mrs. Stössl to serve a meal to the gentlemen if the
family is not in mourning—her mother is very ill. She might even
invite two or three of the gentlemen to stay at her house. The
Quartet will write you again separately. Have a nice vacation.

This is also the first mention of "young Firkušný," then a
piano prodigy of sixteen, of whom more anon. Besides trying to
further the boy's career, Janáček taught him composition, took
him to the opera, and generally treated him like a son—or grand-

son, since their ages were nearly threescore years apart. However, the planned performance never came about.

Janáček was now well enough known throughout musical Europe to be a sitting target for all sorts of unlikely requests. The estimable German daily *Vossische Zeitung* wanted his views (and those of other "well-known composers or other representative foreign musicians") on "What Beethoven means to us today" in fifty lines or less for the centenary of the great man's death. A Berlin paper wanted to know whether the League of Nations should offer a prize for a peace hymn, and whether it should be a march or a cantata; would he please indicate how he saw the rhythm and the melody? Franz Lederer, editor of the *Prager Tagblatt,* tried to persuade Janáček to contribute an article to the Bremen arts magazine *Die Böttchergasse.* The Prague première of Berg's *Wozzeck* had led to a riot and ultimately to the work's withdrawal; to the interviewer from a literary journal, Janáček resolutely defended the composer:

> Injustice—injustice. *Wozzeck* has been wronged, Berg has been grievously wronged. He is a dramatist of great firmness of purpose, profound truth. Let him speak out! Now he is all torn up. He is suffering. As if cut down. Not a note. And his every note was soaked in blood! . . . You ask about the state of opera. Berlin wants to know the same thing. It will advance. . . . Not the crashing of instruments. *Phenomena made plain.* That's its justification. And it will grow with humanity. . . . I get across through *truth.* Truth to the limit. And I believe life has many, many layers; some of them in need of a *beautiful sound,* too— Schreker and Schönberg tend to forget that. Truth does not exclude beauty, on the contrary, we need more and more truth *and* beauty. Above all life. Everlasting youth. Life is ever young. Life is spring. I'm not afraid of life, I love it with a passion!

Janáček was also being besieged by offers of libretti, including one from William Ritter, *Le Château en Bohème,* which featured an aircraft whose propeller Ritter hoped would summon up memories of the clacking millstone at the beginning of *Jenufa.* None of it appealed. Then, on 8 May 1928, a more serious proposal, from the director of Berlin's Renaissance Theater, Gustav

Hartung: Would Janáček be interested in writing incidental music for Gerhart Hauptmann's comedy *Schluck und Jau?* Here was accolade indeed. Hauptmann, a native of Silesia (just over the border from Janáček's home district), was one of the greatest German men of letters of his generation, a writer on social themes, author of the 1892 play *Die Weber* (The Weavers) about the unsuccessful weaver's revolt of 1844, winner of the 1912 Nobel Prize for literature. Hartung was director of the annual *Festspiele* in Heidelberg, which would open that year with a formal address by Hauptmann, followed by a new production of his comedy. The previous year, which was the sesquicentennial of the birth of Heinrich von Kleist, it had been his *Kätchen von Heilbronn,* with music drawn from Weber's opera *Euryanthe*—a great success; what could be more appropriate than having Hauptmann's work staged with music by a distinguished opera composer of *his* day? Hartung offered to travel to Brno to discuss the project. A week later, when he still had not heard from Janáček, Hartung wrote again, adding that Hauptmann also begged Janáček to do it. Then the conductor Otto Klemperer weighed in, with a disingenous reference to a possible German première of the as yet unfinished *From the House of the Dead.*

KLEMPERER TO JANÁČEK, 21 MAY 1928

One of our best stage directors, Gustav Hartung, asks me to write in his behalf. Hartung would so much like to interest you in writing incidental music for Gerhart Hauptmann's *Schluck und Jau.* This work is to be presented at the Heidelberg festival. Hauptmann too would be very pleased if this project would interest you.

I am only a go-between in this matter and ask that you accept my plea favorably.—I hope you are well and that *The House of the Dead* will soon be finished. I hope with all my heart that I can perform this work in Berlin.—

Brod also wrote in support of Hartung's request, pointing out that the play's Silesian ambience would not be altogether foreign to the composer. Janáček replied at once.

JANÁČEK TO BROD, 17 MAY 1928

So you are home again—judging from your letter! Thank

you for remembering me with a postcard [from Jerusalem, which Brod had been visiting for the first time].

I don't know what will come of that *Schluck und Jau.* It will probably founder for lack of time. It's true I write fast, but I polish for a long time. They should have remembered that, rather. I have replied to Mr. Hartung.

I have written a second string quartet: I called it *Intimate Letters.* I'll hear Friday whether it is a better piece than the 1st quartet.

They're taking their time in Berlin with *The Makropulos Affair.*

I'm curious to hear how Palestine affected you.

The *Glagolitic Mass* was well received; it is fierce.

[Bruno] Walter of Berlin is to conduct *Taras Bulba* in London and somewhere else as well.

From the House of the Dead—that will cost me some work yet!

Now I'm off for a few days to finish renovating my cottage in Hukvaldy and just to sit around looking into the good Lord's windows.

The Brno exhibition will be inaugurated with *Katya Kabanova, Jenufa,* and the *Sinfonietta.* All during Whitsun!

Keep well. May we meet again soon.

On 22 May 1928 Brod wrote Janáček once more to send him good wishes on the completion of the Second Quartet and an article entitled "Impressions of Palestine" that Brod had dashed off. He reiterated the importance of the Heidelberg festival and again urged Janáček to take on the assignment; after all, only an overture and a few short entr'actes would be required.

Janáček was tempted. Hauptmann's comedy, subtitled "Spiel zu Scherz und Schimpf mit fünf Unterbrechungen" (A Display to Delight and Dismay with Five Interruptions), was loosely based on the "Induction" to *The Taming of the Shrew,* in which a company of huntsmen out for a lark dress up the tinker and tramp Sly as a nobleman while he sleeps off a drunken spree, with servants and with a page transformed into his lady to attend him; the play proper is then put on by a troupe of itinerant players ostensibly for Sly's diversion, although Shakespeare omits to dispose of him at the end. In Hauptmann's version Sly ("Schlau" in Schlegel and Tieck's classic German translation of

Shakespeare's original) becomes a second tramp named Schluck (Gulp), who takes the page's place as wife to the drunken Jau (Cheer). But Jau grows into his role and becomes quite obnoxious to the upper classes, whereupon the huntsmen give both tramps a sleeping potion and set them back on the road—and all appears to be as before.

Janáček may have had trouble with the broad Silesian dialect in which the two tramps continue to speak even after their transformations; yet Jau's intransigence evidently appealed to the composer, and he marked down for special attention Sly's line "Am I a lord?" ("Bin ich ein Lord?" in Schlegel and Tieck), here transformed into "Ich bin a Ferscht?"—a dialect version of "ein Fürst"—which convulsed Hauptmann's audiences the same way Bernard Shaw's Liza Doolittle was to slay them in *Pygmalion*. Janáček thought he could make something of that. He sketched out a few scenes. These sketches, never completed, would probably have remained quite sparse and economical even if he had worked them out—in the spirit of "less is more"— although that was certainly not what Hartung had in mind: he expected whole set pieces as well as interludes during scene changes, developing into dances. Janáček grumbled, "They want a whole opera from me—a comic opera!" Pity he never completed this commission, if only because it would have been fascinating to see how he composed to a German text. (In the event, the play was put on with incidental music drawn from the works of Smetana.)

On 1 July 1928, two days before his seventy-fourth birthday, Janáček left for his annual "cure" at Luhačovice—to take the waters and to submit to an occasional mudbath. The little spa had come to know him well. His stocky, slightly corpulent figure was a familiar sight as he strode vigorously up and down the promenade in his favorite white raw-silk suit. A shooting stick and a rakish white cap lent him a slightly dandified air. He felt marvelously well, even though his heart was not as strong as it had been. The mudbaths had reduced his rheumatism to an occasional twinge, and the daily exercise in the country air was a wonderful change from town life. Only a few weeks earlier, at the Brno exhibition of contemporary culture, he had been asked to participate in what was then still something of a novelty, the selection of a beauty queen. The entire jury was invited to the reception held in the winner's honor. Everyone remarked how young Janáček seemed in mind and body. William Ritter had come for the exhibition and had brought along a party of Frenchmen, one of whom had a Czech wife. She enlivened the occasion by playing the gypsy and reading people's fortunes from their palms. František Neumann, the chief of Brno's opera and Janáček's great champion, offered his palm to be read; he said all he wanted to know was how long he had to live. The fortune-teller would not say. Neumann persisted. After some hesitation, she told him he would die not more than a year after Janáček. Neumann glanced at the composer, so full of life and energy. "He'll be here another twenty years," he said. "That's good enough for me, too!"

Kamila Stössl's mother had died during Janáček's stay at Luhačovice, of cancer. Kamila was distraught; she feared the same fate awaited her. Her relationship with Janáček had grown much closer, perhaps even intimate. For the first time, they began to address each other in the familiar second person singular. Her husband seemed not to mind too much. Janáček had lent him 30,000 crowns (about $1000) to start an antiques shop in a Prague suburb and had become a valued customer: he had just added another storey to his Hukvaldy cottage and was happily furnishing it with purchases from the shop, against the day when Kamila might come to stay with him. In a will made out a year before, he had left most of his fortune to the division of the University of Brno that had awarded him the honorary doctorate, with a life interest to his wife; he had left Kamila the royalties from *Katya Kabanova* but had noted that codicils were not out of the question. Within twenty-four hours he had added one: royalties from the other operas were to go to Zdenka, Kamila was to get additional royalties from *Diary of a Vanished Man,* and her boys were to share some gold coins he had bought earlier, like a peasant hoarding part of his fortune in a mattress. (Actually, they were in a safe deposit box.) In the codicil, he had noted sarcastically, "They are not my sons," for the benefit of the "curious and slanderous."

As his month in Luhačovice drew to a close, Janáček decided to spend August at Hukvaldy. The alterations to the cottage were done; the upstairs room was furnished. Kamila needed a change of scene after the long travail of her mother's illness and death. Would she spend the month in Hukvaldy with him? To his unbounded delight, she agreed. Janáček nearly went out of his mind with excitement. He became feckless: he no longer cared what other people might think or what his wife might feel. She had known of his passion for Kamila all along—Janáček had made no secret of it before Zdenka. On his way from Luhačovice to Hukvaldy, he stopped in Brno. Kamila was to go from Brno to Hukvaldy by the same train; the relationship would be in the open for all to see at last. On 30 July 1928, Zdenka's birthday, Janáček kissed her good-bye, wished her well, and gently chided her for not marking *his* birthday four weeks before. On arriving in Hukvaldy, he sent her a friendly note: "Arrived safely. The house is merry." Kamila's husband David and their son Rudolf are said to have been of the party—a detail that turns out to be decidedly implausible. David Stössl is supposed to have left on a business trip a couple of days later. In any case, Janáček and Kamila were to have a short week together.

On their return from a Sunday walk, Janáček offered to change his will again, to leave Kamila the cottage and a bit of forestland he had added to his property. She refused. In her matter-of-fact way, she said that she came to Hukvaldy only to visit him and for no other reason. She had been keeping an album for Janáček—her husband had got it for him the previous year—so that Janáček could note down occasional thoughts, verses, even snatches of music. That evening, he jotted down five bars of piano music in it marked *dolce* to which he gave the title *Čekám Tě!* (I Wait for Thee). Then he entered in the album a new codicil to his will. Interest on the principal sum left to the University of Brno would now go to Kamila. He gave her the key to the safe deposit box that contained his original will and noted down her earlier promise (supposedly given him in front of her husband) that she would never remarry. "Thus you have promised, while reading these lines along with me," he wrote.

The following day Janáček caught a cold. According to the account repeated in all the biographies, young Rudolf had got lost in the forest; Janáček had dashed out to look for him, run up a hill, been unable to find him, had run down again and up another—a breezy lookout point with a bench on top—had found himself out of breath and overheated, had taken off his coat, and sat down for a moment. The boy is meanwhile supposed to have turned up of his own accord. The story simply does not ring true; it may well have been concocted to placate public and private sensibilities. (Josef Ritter-Tscherff, who remembers staying with William Ritter in a local inn at the time—they had been invited to stay at Janáček's cottage but had had to wait their turn because he had "another guest"—cannot remember any child being there.) More likely Janáček had become overexcited on finding himself alone with Kamila at last and had indeed become chilled in the wake of some imprudent exertions. He said nothing to Kamila about his indisposition for two days, even took a long walk to fetch his laundry from a washerwoman who lived some distance away. That evening he felt quite ill. His pulse was erratic; he had a fever, an earache, and a sore throat, which a local doctor diagnosed next morning as an inflammation of the middle ear and laryngitis. His condition worsened; a second doctor was called in, then a third. Both feared it was pneumonia—the old man's friend, as the saying went: before the advent of antibiotics, elderly bedridden patients easily fell prey to it and seldom recovered. On Friday Janáček finally consented to being taken to the nearest city hospital, in Moravská Ostrava (Mährisch-Ostrau), where the pneumonia diagnosis was confirmed by X ray. Injections to stimulate his failing heart kept him going. He rallied, asked for pen and ink to make another change in his will in favor of Kamila, who had been taken for a relative and given an adjacent room at the hospital. "I write in my own hand, sound of mind. . . . Of my property, Mrs. Kamila Stössl, honorable woman, is to have the interest on 200,000 crowns [about $6600]. . . ." He reiterated the terms of the codicil he had written into their album. Then he weakened again but reared up once more when the Sisters of Holy Cross who were nursing him suggested that he might want to make his peace with God. "Perhaps you don't know who I am, Sister!" The following morning, on 12 August 1928, he suffered a heart attack, was given a sedative, and died in his sleep.

Kamila had not summoned Zdenka from Brno; now she wired that Janáček was seriously ill. Zdenka learned the full truth only when she discovered that the car that was to take her to Ostrava belonged to a funeral home. The two women met over the body—a frightful encounter. Reluctantly, they rode together to Hukvaldy; there was nothing for it, since Kamila had the keys to the cottage and wanted to hand it over in good order. (None of the accounts contains any further mention of her son or of his whereabouts during this ordeal.) It was the last time the two women were on speaking terms; henceforth, they would meet only as litigants.

That evening, František Neumann stepped in front of the curtain at the Brno opera house after he had conducted the first part of Smetana's *Bartered Bride* and announced the sad news. The performance went on, but the audience held its applause; then cast and audience stood together at the end while Neumann led the orchestra in the funeral march from Beethoven's *Eroica* Symphony. A week later, at the public funeral, he conducted the wonderful final scene from *The Cunning Little Vixen,* of which Janáček had once said, after a particularly successful rehearsal, "You'll have to play that for me when I die." Baritone Arnold Flögl sang the gamekeeper's final words, from Janáček's own libretto: "That's how the world keeps youthful! The life of the forest ever renewed. And the nightingales come back every spring without fail.—And people will walk by and bow their heads so low—they'll understand what bliss, heavenly bliss must have just passed by." Neumann was too moved to make a speech, but many other prominent guests spoke, all in Czech except Brod, who took his courage in his hands to say a few words of farewell in German, "in the name of the many tens of thousands who have had the good fortune to experience your art on German stages." Then Janáček was laid to rest, but not forever; fate had one more indignity in store. The private funeral home had only reluctantly ceded its priority when the city of Brno had insisted on a public ceremony and funeral. Yet after the interment he was discovered to have been buried in a private grave after all, not in the place of honor. Two days later, the coffin had to be unceremoniously moved to the official spot.

Opus posthumus

In 1849 the twenty-eight-year-old Fyodor Mikhaylovich Dostoyevsky and some of his comrades were arrested for their opposition to the harsh regime of Tsar Nicholas I and for belonging
to a socialist circle. They were convicted of being revolutionaries
and were summarily condemned to death. The sentence was
commuted to four years of hard labor, to be followed by service
as privates in the army, but the prisoners were not told of this
reprieve. Dostoyevsky and twenty-one others were led into the
prison yard and bound to stakes to be shot. Then the drummers
beat a tattoo, the mock execution was halted, and the reprieve
was read to the prisoners. (The cruel hoax drove one of them
out of his mind.) Dostoyevsky was sent to a camp near Omsk
and then served several years in a Siberian line regiment. On his
return to Moscow he began publishing a novel in serial form
based on his time in prison, *Notes from the House of the Dead*,
which helped establish him as a major writer. This work, which
some of his contemporaries thought was among his greatest, is
not really a novel but a barely disguised objective account of his
own experiences. It is a piece of brilliant reportage on various
aspects of life in a prison camp—first impressions, encounters
with fellow prisoners, their stories, the camp hospital, holiday
happenings, animals, work outside the camp, the last day in
prison—a scheme well suited to the serial format in which the
book first appeared. One of the work's great merits is an air of
detachment, heightened by the situation of the narrator, Aleksandr Petrovich Goryanchikov, as a gentleman among common
folk and by the author's own position (Dostoyevsky was a doc-

tor's son and a former army officer) as the only political prisoner among criminal offenders. This detachment was not based on artistic considerations alone; it also reflected concern for the censor, who might well have suppressed a more impassioned account. In any case, the author's instinctive approach worked well and brought him the first measure of fame.

An unpromising subject for an opera? At first blush it would seem so. The bland Goryanchikov is not much of a central character. The episodic nature of his story means there is next to no plot. There is no hint of a love interest; and the bleak prospects of the all-male cast of prisoners—many of them lifers—might be expected to create a mood of almost unrelieved gloom. Yet Janáček confidently seized on Dostoyevsky's masterpiece as the basis for a libretto, and equally confidently determined to write it himself. His choice of a Russian theme is scarcely surprising in light of his lifelong Russophile leanings, which had survived the Bolshevik takeover. As to the hurdle of an episodic development—well, he had had to contend with that problem in *The Cunning Little Vixen* and had resolved it brilliantly. The lack of female voices was a bigger obstacle but not an insurmountable one: two of the prisoners' tales about the wrongs they had done their sweethearts could be extended to scenes of some length, and the part of the youngest prisoner—a youth of almost maid-like innocence—could be assigned to a mezzo-soprano. The character of Goryanchikov could be fleshed out if his arrival at the camp and his departure were used to frame the story, and if some of the episodes ascribed by Dostoyevsky to other characters were transferred to him. Such consolidation would be needed in any case in several instances, in the usual process by which a novel or even a play must be compressed into a much shorter libretto. Several characters would have to be left out altogether, including the Jewish prisoner Fomich who had so engaged Janáček's sympathy when he exclaimed over him (*molodets'!*) in his open letter to Brod of 12 February 1927. Other characters are unnamed—they simply surface from the chorus briefly as the Tall Prisoner, Short Prisoner, Old Prisoner, and so on. On the other hand, one of Dostoyevsky's episodes was eminently suited for the stage: two plays put on by the prisoners on a feast day. That would practically write itself; there were successful precedents aplenty for a play within a play in both drama (*Hamlet*) and opera (*Pagliacci*).

Z mrtvého domu, called "Aus einem Totenhaus" by Brod and "From the House of the Dead" in English (although "From a Dead House" would be a more literal translation, and "From a Death-house" a more accurate one), is Janáček's most profound opera and, in the opinion of a growing number of cognoscenti, second in importance only to *Jenufa* among his works. He never saw it performed; nor have many operagoers outside Czechoslovakia and Britain to the present day, although there are several recordings of international caliber. But it is sure to make its way and come to be recognized for what it is: one of the great masterpieces of twentieth-century opera, like Kafka's major works tragically prescient of the labor and concentration camps that were to become the scourge of mankind on a scale that neither Dostoyevsky nor Janáček could have begun to imagine in their darkest hours. That much was evident to at least one observer long before *From the House of the Dead* had been validated by events. Reporting on the work's first Prague performance, Rosa Newmarch commented in the July 1931 issue of *The Chesterian* that "the music is made to say and do terrible things." Half a century before Aleksandr Solzhenitsyn's account of the Gulag Archipelago disclosed how monstrously the prison-camp system had been elaborated by Russia's new rulers, she made the connection between Janáček's music and the mood of the century:

> Is all this stridor and dissonance merely subjective, the nervous exasperation and pent up bitterness of a conscience-stricken man? Or may not Janáček have found some startlingly new methods by which to express despair, cruelty and injustice? Is *The House of the Dead* only a mirror reflecting a sick and senile mind, or a flash-light turned upon such terrible verities as our eyes would prefer to evade: the Siberia of Dostoievsky's time, the Bolshevik labour-camps of today?

Act I starts with Goryanchikov's arrival at the prison camp, still in his city clothes, which drive the drunken commandant to a fury; he mockingly asks what the new prisoner thinks he looks like—a brigand? a vagrant?—and is even more infuriated by Goryanchikov's factual reply that he is a political offender. For this imagined impertinence, the commandant orders the new-comer to suffer a hundred lashes, and the hapless Goryanchikov is dragged off. Some of the prisoners had been teasing a lame eagle; they now let go of him, but the bird remains defiant— "Truly, he's not at all like us!" says one of them—and they break out into a tribute: "Eagle, tsar of the forest!" Skuratov, the camp clown, sings a ditty and does a dance. Another prisoner, Luka, tells his story—how he was one of a dozen Ukrainians in another camp, under another crazed commandant, who thought himself the prisoners' tsar and God; how this blasphemy so infuriated Luka that he knifed the commandant to death; and how he was flogged for it till he was near death himself. In a wonderful ex-ample of Janáček's sense of theater, as Luka vividly evokes this past flogging, Goryanchikov is brought in, staggering from the flogging he has just received. But there is no sentimentality; rather, with an abrupt change in mood, as Luka mournfully con-cludes his tale ("I thought I would die"), the Old Prisoner in-terposes ironically, "A umřels?" (And did ye'?), and the act ends with Luka's furious reply, "Idiot!" as Goryanchikov is led away.

Act II takes place a year later, in the summer. Goryanchikov has befriended the Tartar boy Alyeya and promises to teach him to read and write. The prisoners have completed an assigned task (salvaging a wrecked river barge) and know they will have the rest of the day off; there is to be a show, but first Skuratov tells how he came to be in prison. As a private in the army, he fell in love with a German girl, Louisa, but when he discovered she was also being courted by a middle-aged German watch-maker, he shot him dead, for which he got a life sentence. Now the mood changes abruptly: the prisoners prepare to put on two plays, in which they will take all the parts, accompanied by music through which the composer skillfully conjures up the ten-piece camp band described by Dostoyevsky. The first play is a com-pressed version of the Don Juan story, with Leporello's part taken by the servant Kedril (Cyril). The second is a comic, very Russian pantomime on a theme that goes back at least to the *Thousand and One Nights* and one that had also been used in operas by Musorgsky (*Sorochinsky Fair,* 1874), Tchaikovsky (*The Little Slippers,* 1885), and Ravel (*L'Heure espagnole,* 1911): the faithless wife who conceals from her husband a succession of lovers, the last of whom is again Don Juan. The plays over, most of the prisoners leave, but not before the Young Prisoner makes an assignation with an ugly prostitute—again, a dramatic contrast to the tale of Skuratov's courtship of Louisa. Goryanchikov and Alyeya indulge in a cup of tea, a luxury resented by the Short Prisoner; there is a scuffle and Alyeya is injured.

Act III is in two scenes. The first takes place in the camp hospital. Goryanchikov has been reading the Bible to the feverish Alyeya, a Moslem who is greatly impressed with the teachings of Jesus. The braggard Luka lies dying. Another prisoner, Shapkin, now tells his story: how he was arrested for vagrancy and burglary, how he was mistaken for a long-eared scribe wanted for embezzlement, and how the district gendarme nearly pulled his ears off during the interrogation. The other prisoners, greatly excited by this tale, finally simmer down as darkness falls. Now follows the longest story of all, told by the prisoner Shishkov and punctuated by the dying Luka's sighs. Shishkov courted a rich man's daughter, Akulina, after she had been jilted by one Filka Morozov, who had bragged that he had slept with her and had egged on his drinking companions to tar her gate, the peasants' mark of dishonor. Akulina was beaten by her father and locked up and publicly ridiculed by Filka and his mates, of whom Shishkov was one. But his heart wasn't in it: he had fallen in love with her himself and, realizing that no one else would have her, had proposed and been accepted. On their wedding night she was found to have remained virtuous—but the wicked Filka kept on maligning her and suggested that Shishkov must have been drunk to think his bride a maid. Finally, Filka enlisted in the army and had a change of heart: he apologized to Akulina before all the village, and she forgave him—an act that enraged her new husband, especially after Akulina stoutly declared that she had always loved Filka and loved him still. This confession drove Shishkov to a murderous fury. The next day he took his young wife away to a lonely spot and cut her throat. As Shishkov ends his narrative, Luka dies, and Shishkov now recognizes him as his nemesis, Filka—a somewhat implausible turn of events. "Yet a mother bore him, too!" cries the Old Prisoner, and the scene ends with the guards calling for Goryanchikov. The second scene is in the same setting as Act I. Goryanchikov is about to be discharged; the commandant grows maudlin and self-importantly asks his pardon for having maltreated him. Goryanchikov's fetters are struck off. Alyeya bids him a tearful farewell; the Tall Prisoner releases the eagle, his wing healed, and the bird flies off; and the guards relentlessly order the prisoners back to work. They shuffle off, their fetters clanging rhythmically, as the curtain falls.

All the references in Janáček's correspondence pertaining to this opera go to show how much it took out of him. "I am finishing off one piece of work after another, as if I meant to put paid to life," he wrote Kamila Stössl on 30 November 1927. "I rush the new opera along like a baker shoves loaves into the oven!" A few days later he continued, "I'm coming to the end of what will be perhaps my greatest work—this latest opera. I got so agitated my blood like to have gushed out." Earlier, he had written her: "It is giving me lots of hard work, this black opera of mine; in it I feel I am going down step by step, lower and lower, down to the very bottom of the most wretched of all mankind. And it is heavy going." It is not clear when he came to the end of his travail. On 10 January 1928 he had reported to Brod, "I am finished with Dostoyevsky's *From the House of the Dead*. The score is already being copied. . . . This year [1927] has been like a soul in fire." But in his last letter to Brod, on 17 May 1928, he wrote, "*From the House of the Dead*—that will cost me some work yet!" Two weeks before that he had a distinct premonition of the approaching end.

Janáček to Kamila Stössl, 5 May 1928

I feel strongly that it's high time I laid down my pen. You can't imagine what a weight off my mind it will be when this *House of the Dead* is finished. This is the third year it has haunted me, night and day. And I still don't know what it will turn out to be. I just pile note upon note; and the Tower of Babel grows. When it collapses on me I'll be buried.

Janáček had indeed been thinking for several years about using Dostoyevsky's book, which he had read both in the Russian original and in a Czech translation. During his trip to London in 1926 he had started to write a violin concerto, to be called "A Soul's Pilgrimage." Some of the musical themes he had sketched out for it found their way into the opera—two extended lyrical passages that stand out in this harshly masculine work— at the close of the overture and again near the end of the last act. (The predominance of male voices—a problem that had also plagued Puccini in *The Girl of the Golden West*—is somewhat softened by the imitations of the direct speech of various characters in the prisoners' tales, for which Janáček went so far as to write interjections in a different clef; and of course by Alyeya's role being sung by a mezzo-soprano.) Janáček told no one of his project at first. "He meant to make a secret of his work," remarks the editor of the Janáček–Brod correspondence, "but his intent was frustrated by an indiscretion." No further details are given, but there is a letter among the Löwenbach papers in San Diego from which it appears that the disclosure probably came about through Olin Downes. Janáček had renewed his acquaintance with the American critic during the trip to Frankfurt for the fifth ISCM festival in 1927. "Downes in Frankfurt was the first whom Janáček told he was doing *From the House of the Dead*," wrote Mrs. Löwenbach from New York to Ivo Stolařík in Opava in 1958. "No one in Prague knew anything about it before that."

And when did Janáček finish the opera, if he ever did? His autograph score was so sparsely orchestrated in places as to give the impression that it was a piece of chamber music—or else a rough sketch for a subsequent fuller orchestration. This impression was the stronger because the score was not written on sheets of regular upright notepaper, with perhaps twenty staves printed on both sides, as were Janáček's other operas. Instead, it resembled some of his orchestral compositions in that it was written on blank sheets of paper, laid on their sides, on which Janáček *drew* the staves freehand, leaving them off wherever instruments

"A umřels?" (And did ye' [die]?), the Old Prisoner's ironic
query in Act I of *From the House of the Dead* in Janáček's
autograph.

or voices were silent and resuming the lines in mid-page as
needed. That was evidently how he had started to write the violin
concerto; when it became the overture of the opera, he just
continued in that format and on the same kind of paper. A fair
copy was then made from this autograph score, a job that was
finished on 23 May 1928, a week after Janáček had written Brod
that the opera would cost him some work yet. In fact he spent
another month on it, making further adjustments and additions
and perhaps again dictating some of the simpler changes (such
as instrumental doublings and octaves) to the copyists, Václav
Sedláček and Jaroslav Kulhánek. But on 19 June 1928 Janáček
wrote Kamila that the copyists would be done the next day. Still
he was not completely satisfied. He reworked parts of the fair
copy of the first two acts during July at Luhačovice; and he took
the third act with him on that last stay at Hukvaldy, where it
was found, unchanged, after his death.

These circumstances—especially the sparse orchestration—
misled the man charged with bringing the work to performance,
the Brno theater director Ota Zítek, into believing that he was
dealing with an incomplete version. He engaged two of Janáček's
former students, the conductor Břetislav Bakala and the composer Osvald Chlubna, to fill out the orchestration and to provide a new ending, much as Franco Alfano had done four years
earlier for an opera that really did lack a finale, Puccini's *Turan-
dot*. The latter is now invariably performed with Alfano's ending, which nevertheless did not impress the conductor of the
opera's première, Arturo Toscanini: he simply stopped the work
when he came to the end of Puccini's score, turned to the audience, and said, "Here the Master laid down his pen"—an attitude Zítek would have been wise to emulate, especially since
a perfectly good ending was in hand. Instead, he undertook to
edit the libretto. The changes penciled in by Chlubna and Bakala
on the Sedláček–Kulhánek fair copy do not accord with Janáček's mature style, which is so unique as to be inimitable. Indeed, he is supposed to have remarked once to his composition
students, "Please don't ape me, I don't care for Janáčekisms;
there is only one Janáček—and that's me."

In their effort to make the work more suitable for the opera
house, Chlubna and Bakala did not merely double many instrumental parts (which Janáček might have done himself if he had
lived to attend the rehearsals), they also thickened the texture
with more brass and woodwinds, added a gratuitous harp, and
generally romanticized the sound. But Zítek's rankest offense
was to change the endings of the first and last acts. In the first
act, he interpolated an abortive attempt by Goryanchikov to as-
sassinate the commandant—an episode that Dostoyevsky assigned to a hardened criminal, not the blameless Goryanchikov,
and that is in no way shown in the music. How Janáček would
have hated that is evident from his violent reaction (in his letter
of 9 November 1926) to Brod's suggestion about the stage business with the envelope near the end of *The Makropulos Affair*:
"I should have to reflect that action in the music and I'm not
going to." Worse still, Zítek changed the uncompromisingly terse
finale of the opera—Goryanchikov's release while the hopeless
life of the prison goes on unrelenting—to make it end on a more

optimistic and elevating note: a short hymn to freedom sung by the prisoners, with an accompaniment patched together from several bars of Janáček's own music. It is safe to assume that this was *not* Janáček's intent. He was not trying to emulate Beethoven's *Fidelio,* another opera about a prison, which does end with a hymn sung by the released prisoners. If he had any model in mind at all, it would have been Berg's *Wozzeck,* which he so admired and which also expresses deepest compassion for the powerless without once sinking into sentimentality.

Nevertheless, it was this revised version that Zítek directed and Bakala conducted at the première in Brno on 12 April 1930, that Universal Edition published, that was widely performed throughout Germany (in Brod's translation) before the Second World War, and that survived into further postwar performances, including the first performance heard in Britain (at the 1964 Edinburgh Festival by the Prague National Theater). Yet not everyone was happy with it. Jaroslav Vogel, Janáček's biographer and the conductor of a new production at the National Theater in Prague on 10 May 1958, made the first break with the Bakala–Chlubna version when he restored Janáček's original ending: he thought it was dramatically more consistent, though perhaps less effective dynamically and structurally than the revision—and since something was to be said for both versions, he felt the composer's intent ought to be honored. But the main pressure for restoration came about as musical opinion and public taste developed to a point at which they had so to speak caught up with Janáček. In 1961 the Czech-born conductor Rafael Kubelík (son of the world-famous violin virtuoso Jan Kubelík) conducted a concert version in Munich in which most of Bakala and Chlubna's additions were deleted and the orchestration followed the original autograph score, and which was also brought out by Universal Edition; it was staged by the English National Opera in 1965. And in 1980 Sir Charles Mackerras, in collaboration with the British musicologist and Janáček specialist John Tyrrell, prepared a version based on the even more authentic Sedláček–Kulhánek copy containing Janáček's own amendments, which was used in the definitive recording (without Bakala and Chlubna's additions) that Mackerras made with the Vienna Philharmonic and Czech singers. The liner notes include a speculation on whether it might not be in part the growing sophistication of audiences that makes the opera so effective despite its disdain for operatic conventions. Tyrrell writes:

> Part of the answer is to be found in the single-minded commitment that Janáček brought to the work, resulting in music more intense, dissonant and powerfully charged than in any previous work of his. Its highly original, almost cinematic construction (perfecting a model he had tried out with varying success in *Fate, Brouček,* and the *Vixen*), allowed him to absorb in it different worlds, with quite disparate elements. In it, despite its grim framework, mingle the lyricism of *Kaťa,* the humor and the wisdom of the *Vixen,* the mixture of the mundane and the fantastic of *Makropulos.* It was a fitting and glorious culmination of his life's work. Far ahead of its time, the opera was an embarrassment to his contemporaries, and even to Janáček's pupils, who softened its harsh musical speech and distorted its uncompromising message. Only today are we in the position to hear it in its true guise and perhaps comprehend its importance.

And what of Brod? For once he could not rely on Janáček to straighten him out when he strayed too far from the composer-librettist's intent. Brod made one significant improvement in the staging: he placed the first act in the wintertime and the second in summer—an effect that can be heightened still further if the beginning of the second act is set at midday and the opera's end at sunrise. In an article published in the *Prager Tagblatt* of 30 July 1930 and also reproduced as a postscript to the translated libretto that Universal Edition published in 1930, Brod wrote at length of his relationship with Janáček:

> I have come to the end of this text translation and my friend is dead; he cannot help me as he had helped me with the translations of all his opera texts. There is no one to consult. How briskly the letters used to fly between Prague and Brno whenever a passage was not clear, whenever Janáček proposed amendments. In a great many cases he took my objections into account; how often did we meet for long and agitated discussions to settle on the definitive version. In *The Cunning Little Vixen* in particular my translation really became a poetic recasting. A simple

comparison between the German and Czech texts makes it plain in how many instances line after line has been changed in that opera, in my view the Master's deepest and most original work, one that is still not properly appreciated. Of course not a single one of these alterations, all intended to clarify meaning and action and their underlying assumptions, was made without Janáček's approval. In the end he was so pleased with the outcome of our collaboration that he expressly asked for a foreign-language production to be based on the German and not on the original Czech text.

It is this collaboration that I miss so bitterly. I had to face the text of this posthumous work alone for the first time. My great friend is dead. I feel the full weight of responsibility on my shoulders.

That a text revision (whether major or minor in extent) became necessary whenever Janáček brought an opera to me—that was the result of his insistence on writing his own libretti. He drew his dramatic inspiration in the most direct way from a book, a play, or a novel; as he read (including the *House of the Dead*) he marked the passages that struck him; he took over some things verbatim but in snatches, yet at the same time omitted interconnections quite heedlessly, while combining characters and situations that he sensed were related. One might say he composed the omitted passages along with the rest; they remain invisible to the theater audience, yet are manifest in his sensibility, though not outwardly. The result is that many an episode has a meaning that differs somewhat from the literal. One must carefully scan the original work on which the composer drew to get down to the truest meaning that Janáček expresses in his passionate music, without worrying pedantically about every detail of the textual substrate.

This method has its advantages. The larger concept, the immediacy and unity of Janáček's operatic creations, often could not have been achieved if the composer had not absolutely pounced on the text wildly and heedlessly in order to make it his own in his altogether personal way.

To limit the disadvantages of this method by careful reconstruction of the underlying text after the fact—that is what I have considered to be an essential task of my recasting. Another person who should undertake such a reconstruction is the stage director, who can scarcely hope to do a good job of staging the *House of the Dead* without a thorough knowledge of Dostoyevsky's work. In many instances Dostoyevsky's *From the House of the Dead* reads like an illuminating gloss on Janáček's extremely sparse text. Since Janáček is gone, Dostoyevsky's book has been my only adviser in the creation of the new textual formulation.

I have used the [German] translation of Moeller van den Bruck (published by Piper) and have referred to the Russian original in cases of doubt. Peculiar errors, doubtless oversights caused by haste, especially in the spelling of proper names, have been corrected. Where Janáček deliberately deviates from Dostoyevsky I naturally had to follow Janáček. It is curiously hard to draw the line. "He stands there like a mammoth," Janáček has it. "Like a monument," says Dostoyevsky's prisoner. Did Janáček misread it or change it intentionally? I left it at "mammoth."

I did not feel justified in blunting the way Janáček lets Dostoyevsky's characters almost universally slide into a heavy, dead earnest, deeply black atmosphere. In Dostoyevsky there is a marvellous aura of semidarkness, a curious indifference and occasionally even a false gaiety of the prisoners, a humanly extremely complex floating mood that sometimes seems to palliate the account's dreadfulness momentarily and even to suspend it, but in reality and in overall impression serves to enhance it till it is almost unbearable—precisely because of its humanity and shading. The colors of Janáček's palette are in the main submerged in a more uniform and simpler murkiness. For example, Janáček's opening name-calling scene ("What sort of bird are you? . . . "This sort!" . . . "What sort?" etc.) is in Dostoyevsky's account a mere pretense at comedy of a sort the prisoners indulge in for their amusement—though a dismayingly rough amusement. The stage manager may perhaps realize this characteristic twilight of the prison camp successfully in various passages. Even Skuratov, Dostoyevsky's jester, becomes a tragic figure when seen through the medium of Janáček's agitated music. Of course I kept to Janáček's intent absolutely in such striking cases. But I thought I might strengthen Alyeya's role somewhat by going back to Dostoyevsky's figure, for his characteristics are quite strongly reflected in Janáček's music but only weakly in the wording of the text. So there were many moments when I missed Janáček's resistance, his opposition, and his consent most dreadfully again and again.

The work is done. And now I look back on the twelve years during which it was given to me to work with and for Janáček.

It began the moment I found myself wedged into the packed gallery standing room at the National Theater in Prague listening to *Jenufa,* the music of a composer wholly unknown abroad, appreciated only by a few at home, derided as a freak by the hacks. My heart was instantly captivated by those rhythms, not only simple and natural but also laden with a new kind of power of strong sensibility. And I count it as one of my life's great blessings that I was able to find Janáček (who was already 62 at the time *Jenufa* was first produced in Prague) and that I could help him gain his present unquestioned general recognition. With the translation of his *opus posthumus* I come to the end of a labor that encompasses, besides several essays, the translation of *Jenufa, Katya Kabanova, The Cunning Little Vixen, The Makropulos Affair,* the indescribably beautiful *Diary of a Vanished Man,* several songs and choral works, as well as my monograph *Leoš Janáček.* The work is complete but it is not done—for the significance of Janáček, however highly he may be esteemed, is still not appreciated in its entirety; his choral works for example are all too little known and German opera houses have so far not seen fit to bring to life the Panic sensuality and all the innocent and joyful pagan enchantment of his tale of forests and animals, *The Cunning Little Vixen.*

The greatness and power of the *House of the Dead,* which is in some respects a dark counterpart of the joyful *Vixen,* disclose once more the full force of an elemental creative personality in whose immeasurable depths cold, bloodnumbing terror slumbered alongside childlike fond play, both of them inborn and familiar to the demoniac man who here and there brought them forth to limn them as sounds. Through a careful hearing one might gather from the look and expression of the living man something of the great silence of eternity.

Apotheosis

The rest of the story is soon told. Janáček's personal circle dissolved quickly after his death. Within the first year František Neumann was gone, just as the sham gypsy had prophesied, dead at fifty-five: at a *Don Giovanni* rehearsal, he had become overheated and had caught a cold that developed into pneumonia—the same sequence that had caused Janáček's death. David Stössl persuaded his wife to sue the Janáček estate for the bequests that Janáček had specified in their album, which were recognized neither by Zdenka nor by his own relatives, and complex and prolonged litigation not unlike that in *The Makropulos Affair* ensued: the family's attorneys sought to show that the codicils had been written under conditions of "uncontrollable psychic incitement," whereas Kamila's lawyer depicted his client as a woman who had repeatedly tried to end her friendship with a man who had been so much in the public eye, with the concomitant potential for scandal, yet at the same time "had known how to banish the banality and tedium of the life he led in his own home." Materials to show that she had indeed been his "muse and inspiration" were not lacking: not a few of the nearly seven hundred letters she had received from Janáček were impassioned testimonials to his feelings for her. The court recognized most of the Stössls' claim, but they did not enjoy their inheritance for long. Kamila, her worst forebodings fulfilled, died of cancer at forty-three in 1935; David emigrated to America. Zdenka Janáček died three years later, in 1938. The bulk of Janáček's estate then reverted to the University of Brno, which eventually set up a museum and a center for Janáček studies.

After the 1930 Brno première of *From the House of the Dead*, the opera was performed in Prague and in several German houses, notably at the Kroll Theater in Berlin (where Klemperer was *Opernchef*), under the same conductor who had directed the Berlin première of *Katya Kabanova,* Fritz Zweig; he later put together a suite consisting of the overture, the plays within the play, and the opera's finale that he performed on several occasions, including one in London in 1937. Janáček had died in the tenth year of Czechoslovakia's existence; during the next ten years—which was all the time that remained before the republic was dismembered—Janáček's reputation grew only slowly. *Jenufa* continued to be popular, but the other operas fared less well. The splendid new production of *The Cunning Little Vixen* (with a proper children's chorus and ballet) that Václav Talich mounted in Prague in 1937 did little to help establish the work. The following year—the tenth anniversary of Janáček's death—brought a brief quickening of interest. Two young pianists gave all-Janáček recitals in Prague. The first was Walter Susskind, then twenty-four, of whose playing at his debut recital in 1930 Brod had written that it brought Walter Gieseking to mind. Susskind also studied composition with Fidelio Finke and Alois Hába, contributed to Hába's contemporary-music monthly *Rytmus* published by the ISCM's Czechoslovak section, and was already a prominent member of the country's artistic avant-garde (see Appendix). His recital program consisted of most of the Janáček solo piano works and the Concertino, which he conducted from the piano. (He was also one of George Szell's assistants and ultimately turned entirely to conducting.) The recital was such a success that it had to be repeated. The other young pianist was the twenty-six-year-old Rudolf Firkušný, a former child prodigy who had made his concert debut with the Czech Philharmonic at the age of ten and who had been Janáček's composition pupil and protégé. His program likewise included the Concertino, but he also performed the Capriccio for left hand and chamber orchestra, which was conducted by Karel Ančerl, another Hába student and *Rytmus* contributor.

The rise of interest in Janáček occasioned by the activities of that generation of young artists came to an abrupt halt with the Munich pact in the autumn of 1938. The Sudeten, Bohemia's

Leoš Janáček:

Příhody Lišky Bystroušky

Opera o 3 dějstvích v 9 obrazech dle R. Těsnohlídkovy „Lišky Bystroušky".

Řídí: **Václav Talich** — Jevištní provedení: **Luděk Mandaus**

Revírník	Josef Křikava	Cvrček	Jiří Hromas
Paní revírníková	Marie Veselá	Kobylka	Božena Schwörová
Rechtor	Jaroslav Gleich	Skokánek	Jan Plavka
Farář	Josef Celerin	Datel	Marie Pixová
Harašta, obchodník drůbeží	Jan Konstantin	Komár	Františka Lavičková
Pásek, hostinský	Theodor Schütz	Jezevec	Josef Celerin
Bystrouška	Marja Tauberová	Sova	Dobroslava Sudíková
Pásková, hostinská	Božena Kozliková	Sojka	Milada Ševcovicová
Lišák	Ota Horáková	Modrá vážka	Helena Smirnová
Malá Bystrouška	Hana Krausová	•	
Frantík ⎱ kluci	Marta Beranová	Slepičky, Lišky, Lesní havěť.	
Pepík ⎰	Táňa Tomanová	I. Suchý žleb. — II. Myslivna. — III. Doupě jezevcovo. —	
Lapák, pes	Štěpánka Štěpánová	IV. Hospoda u Pásků. — V. Cestou z hospody. — VI. Ná-	
Kohout	Anna Kejřová	mluvy. — VII. Smrt. — VIII. Zahrada u Pásků. — IX. Suchý	
Chocholka, slípka	Marie Barvitiusová	žleb.	

Technická spolupráce: **Jelizaveta Nikolská, Zdenka Hoffmeisterová** a **Kamil Vltouš**
Dětské sbory studoval J. Kühn a zpívá dětský sbor Radiojournalu.
Dětský balet ze školy Jelizavety Nikolské.

Po druhém a šestém obraze přestávka. Mezi představením přístup do hlediště zakázán.

Národní divadlo:

Sobota 22. V. o 15 hod.: **Čert a Káča** Pro školní mládež
Pixová, Kozlíková, Janík, Munclingr, Thein, řídí Škvor

Sobota 22. V. o 19½ hod.: **Lazebník sevillský** (mimo)
Taťana Menotti j. h., Kozlíková, Chorovič, Otava, Thein, Celerin,
řídí Škvor

Neděle 23. V. o 15½ hod.: **Prodaná nevěsta**
Kočová, Blažíček, Kratěk j. h., Celerin, řídí Škvor
Pro Alšovu jednotu republikánského dorostu

Neděle 23. V. o 20 hod.: **Prodaná nevěsta**
Horáková, Berlik, Gleich, Zítek, řídí Václav Talich

Pondělí 24. V. o 19½ hod.: **Příhody Lišky Bystroušky** (mimo)
Tauberová, Horáková, Křikava, řídí Václav Talich

Úterý 25. V. o 19½ hod.: **Bílá nemoc** (mimo)

Středa 26. V. o 15 hod.: **Prodaná nevěsta** Pro školní mládež
Zd. Jurová j. h., Berlik, Kratěk j. h., Mandaus, řídí Škvor

Středa 26. V. o 19½ hod.: **Příhody Lišky Bystroušky** (mimo)
Tauberová, Horáková, Křikava, řídí Václav Talich

Taťana MENOTTI

Sobota 22. V.:

Lazebník sevillský

Playbill for Václav Talich's May 1937 production of *The Cunning Little Vixen,* with the Prague broadcast station's children's chorus and dancers from Jelizaveta Nikolská's ballet school for children.

strategic borderlands, were incorporated into the Third Reich. Musical activities slowed to a trickle: *inter arma silent musæ.* The German opera house in Prague closed its doors after a brilliant half-century, never to reopen (it is now the Smetana Theater); its conductors—Szell, Rudolf, Zweig—left the country. Susskind was on a concert tour of Holland when the rest of Bohemia and Moravia became a German "protectorate" in March 1939. Firkušný made his way to Paris and then to New York. These young men ultimately became the ambassadors who carried Janáček's name to the larger world. Of those who remained home, Ančerl spent most of the Second World War in concentration camps, the only member of his family to survive. Rafael Kubelík, who briefly succeeded Václav Talich as conductor of the Czech Philharmonic, could not do very much for Janáček while the country was under the Nazi yoke. (Both men ultimately continued their careers abroad: Kubelík in Chicago, London, and Munich; and Ančerl, who stayed on in Prague until 1969, in Toronto.)

Rudolf Firkušný had been brought to Janáček's attention as a five-year-old prodigy. Janáček overcame his usual suspicion of the most common type of wunderkind—the skillful freak that manifestly lacks the talent and musical intelligence to weather the transition to adult performer—and listened to the child, pronounced him to be genuinely talented, and took charge of his musical education. He sent him to study piano with Ludmila Tučková (the pianist who had saved most of Janáček's sonata *1. X. 1905* for posterity by secretly copying it) and later with Vilém Kurz; he taught him composition; and he took him about in the wider world, including the Brno premières of *Katya,* the *Vixen,* and *The Makropulos Affair,* at one of which the boy first met Brod. Janáček continued to champion Firkušný to the very end, when he tried to include him in the concert at Písek at which the Second Quartet would have been first performed had Janáček lived. Firkušný in his turn became an indefatigable champion of Janáček's piano music (including the *Fairytale* for cello and piano and the Violin Sonata, as well as the virtuoso piano part in *The Diary of a Vanished Man*), much of which he had played for Janáček, so that his recordings of it are the most authentic. The debt Firkušný owed Janáček was amply repaid when the young prodigy turned into an internationally known pianist and later a teacher at the Juilliard School of Music in New York, where he undertook to interest his students and fellow faculty members in Janáček's music. (He also frequently performed and advanced the cause of the largely unknown piano music of Smetana and what little was written for the piano by Dvořák, whose somewhat clumsy Piano Concerto he recorded in 1975 with the Saint Louis Symphony under Walter Susskind.) Firkušný's persistence has paid off, even in countries to whose musical traditions Janáček's music is especially foreign, such as Italy. Early in Firkušný's career he had somewhat incongruously included a first performance of Janáček's Concertino in an orchestral concert in Rome at the request of the conductor, Bernardino Molinari, and had received the first boos of his career for his pains; on the poster outside the Augusteum announcing the Italian première—*Prima esecuzione in Italia*—a disgruntled subscriber had scribbled, *e anche ultima* (and also the last). Yet four decades later the same pianist was asked to include three all-Janáček recitals in an Italian tour. No one has done more for the world renown of Janáček's nonoperatic output than Firkušný, not even the several Czech quartets that play Janáček's two quartets wherever they go. (One of them, founded in 1947 by the late Jiří Trávníček, adopted the name Janáček Quartet in 1949.)

Of Firkušný's contemporaries, Gabor Otvos conducted *The Makropulos Affair* at the New York City Opera in 1970, and Walter Susskind in 1976. Its American première took place at the San Francisco Opera, another early Janáček stronghold, in 1966; besides that work and a 1969 *Jenufa,* San Francisco heard a *Katya Kabanova* conducted by Kubelík, who also produced the aforementioned concert version of *From the House of the Dead* in Munich in 1961 and New York in 1983. (Kubelík and Susskind had been friends since their student days in Prague: at Susskind's graduation from the piano master class, with a performance of the Schumann Piano Concerto, Kubelík had been concertmaster of the Conservatory orchestra.) But the postwar period also saw the rise of a new Janáček champion, a musician not from Czechoslovakia at all but from the other side of the world.

The new star was a young American-born Australian,

Charles Mackerras, who had hit upon the original plan of soaking up European musical traditions in Prague, despite the linguistic obstacles it presented. Mackerras decided he would study conducting with Václav Talich, so he doggedly learned Czech and then went to Prague on a one-year British Council scholarship. In 1948 he returned to London rather than remain in Czechoslovakia after the Communist takeover, which had resulted in a polarization between partisans of the Smetana-Fibich-Foerster-Jeremiáš-Ostrčil school and the Dvořák-Suk-Novák-Martinů succession. Mackerras came away with a boundless admiration for Janáček (who had belonged to no school), settled in Britain, and later came to play a prime role in fashioning the English National Opera. The company was the former Sadler's Wells Opera (with elements of the still older Carl Rosa Opera), which had closed its doors during the Second World War but had then brilliantly resumed its career in 1945 with the world première of Benjamin Britten's *Peter Grimes* and had been the first in Britain to stage *Katya Kabanova, The Cunning Little Vixen, The Makropulos Affair,* and (later) *From the House of the Dead.* In 1968 the company moved from the Sadler's Wells Theater in north London to the Coliseum in the West End, and Mackerras became the musical director. In 1974 the name was changed to the English National Opera, and in 1979 Mackerras was knighted. (He had also received the Janáček Medal from the Czechoslovak government.) Through his frequent performances and broadcasts of Janáček operas on both sides of the Atlantic, as well as a series of splendid recordings, Sir Charles has probably brought Janáček operas to more listeners than any other conductor.

Another great Janáček specialist is the Swedish soprano Elisabeth Söderström, who has appeared as Jenufa, Katya, and Elina Makropulos from London to San Francisco and has frequently recorded with Mackerras. And among the latest generation of top Janáček interpreters are Britain's prodigiously talented Simon Rattle, who first conducted *The Cunning Little Vixen* at the Glyndebourne Festival Opera in 1977, when he was twenty-two; and Richard Armstrong, who has led whole cycles of Janáček operas at both the Welsh National and Scottish National Operas.

As to Max Brod. He remained in Prague until the day before the German troops entered it. Armed with one of the ten family immigration permits for Palestine (then administered by Britain under a League of Nations mandate) that were all the Chamberlain government had made available to Prague's Jewish community, Brod and his wife crossed over into Poland—at Ostrava, where Janáček had died—literally minutes before the occupation troops sealed the frontier. As a prominent anti-Nazi, he was on the arrest list that had been efficiently compiled months before, and in fact the Gestapo came looking for him in Prague later that day; he had narrowly escaped certain death. (His brother, sister-in-law, and niece were not so lucky: they were all murdered by the Nazis.) Brod and his wife made their way to the Black Sea harbor of Constantsa in Rumania, where they took a ship for Tel Aviv. Shortly after their arrival, he was engaged as the dramaturge of the Habima Theater, a "method" ensemble originally active in Moscow (during the early years of the Bolshevik regime) with the support of Maksim Gorki and Konstantin Stanislavski. He held the job for many years, even after the state of Israel was formed in 1948. It was also during these years that Brod became a world figure, following the translation of his Kafka biography into English in 1947, which led to international recognition of Kafka as a major writer and thinker. (Like Janáček's *From the House of the Dead,* Kafka's works—notably *The Trial* and *The Castle*—are seen by some critics as anticipations of the totalitarian excesses of the twentieth century.) Brod's interpretation of his friend's work and life, long regarded as controversial, has come to be increasingly accepted in recent years. His faith in the importance of Kafka's work has been most thoroughly vindicated, as has his faith in Janáček. The music critic and translator Andrew Porter, writing in *The New Yorker* on 24 November 1980, aptly summarized how the world had come to regard Janáček's chef d'oeuvre during the three-quarters of a century since its première:

> *Jenufa*—does it still need saying? is one of the great operas of our century. Suffering and despair have not been more keenly shared. Attending it is a searing experience. Poor little Butterfly

draws easy, enjoyable tears; *Jenufa* is drama and music on another level. It would be unbearable but for the composer's tenderness and compassion. Out of the tragedy and the horror, understanding and love are born.

Peter Docherty's cover of program booklet for English National Opera's *Brouček*.

Since then, the San Francisco Opera has mounted a performance (with Elisabeth Söderström as Jenufa) in Czech; the New York City Opera has done a nationwide telecast of *The Cunning Little Vixen,* a production designed by the book illustrator Maurice Sendak; Mackerras has conducted *Brouček*; and Simon Rattle has conducted a concert performance of Janáček's early opera *Fate,* which not even Brno had heard until 1958. (In what Andrew Porter called "Janáček-thirsty Britain," there had already been isolated performances of *Šárka* and of *The Beginning of a Romance.*) One would do well to consider Edith Sitwell's strictures, first published in 1929 in her *Tradition and Experiment in Present-day Literature,* and cited by Rosa Newmarch over fifty years ago, apropos of her review of *From the House of the Dead*:

> When we consider the realm of new poetry, or of newness, and consequent strangeness in any of the arts—let us remember that the irritation felt by people contemplating this newness has been felt by each generation towards the pioneer artists of their time. . . . This queer irritating substance when it becomes, as it will become automatically, a classic, will be so known, that future generations will take its beauty for granted without worrying about it.

As our tale concludes, in Brod's centenary year, we honor the memory of the man who was not only the first to recognize the genius of the great artists who crossed his path, but also the one who through his own initiative and enterprise assured that they would have their chance in the wider world. Janáček would have lacked all incentive to write his last four operas if *Jenufa* had met with no response abroad. That it achieved international renown betimes was due to Brod's intervention. In his *Max Brod: Ein Portrait,* Berndt Wessling records what Alma Mahler-Werfel said about Brod: "Without him, what would Janáček have become? A nonentity, a composer who still would have been scarcely known even within the borders of his homeland." Rudolf Firkušný has said it more aptly: "Without Max Brod, Leoš Janáček's world reputation would not have arrived for many more years."

MAX BROD

HEINRICH HEINE

*Meinem lieben
Landsmann, dem*

„Wer nicht so weit geht, als sein Herz
ihn drängt und die Vernunft ihm er-
laubt, ist eine Memme; wer weiter geht,
als er gehen wollte, ist ein Sklave."
                        HEINRICH HEINE
„Die Gipfel sehen einander."

*wundervollen Dirigenten
W. Süßkind
herzlichst
Max Brod
1957*

NON STOP-BÜCHEREI

BERLIN-GRUNEWALD

Title page of Brod's 1935 biography of Heinrich Heine (reissued in 1956 for the centenary of the poet's death), with dedication to Walter Susskind.

Appendix: WALTER SUSSKIND
ON JANÁČEK

The following two excerpts exemplify the impassioned enthusiasm with which the new generation of progressive Czech artists regarded Janáček's music during the decade following his death. The excerpts are from volume 3 (1937–38) of the avant-garde Czech music journal *Rytmus* edited by Alois Hába. The first passage (pp. 45–46) is an advance program note for a 14 December 1937 all-Janáček concert conducted by Karel Ančerl in which Otakar Hollmann played the Capriccio and Walter Susskind the Concertino, and the Prague Quartet played the Second Quartet, "Intimate Letters." The second passage is the first part of a three-part essay on Janáček—Bartók—de Falla, three "folklorist" composers whose works happened to be getting extensive hearings in that last Prague spring before the Munich agreement ended the Czechoslovak capital's role as prewar Europe's prime center of contemporary music. (An introductory comment lambasts composers whose approach to folklore consists of "the use of folk elements and cheap quotations of entire folksongs in works whose only objective is profit and gain," an obvious reference to the light opera *Schwanda the Bagpiper* by Jaromír Weinberger, whom Brod for some reason admired but the avant-garde despised.)

1

I marvel at the thousands upon thousands of manifestations of rhythms, of worlds of light, of color, of sound and touch, and my tone grows young through the eternal rhythmic renewal of eternally young nature.

"My tone grows young . . ."—seldom has a composer more aptly captured the essence of his artistic personality and development than has Leoš Janáček by this sentence. In fact his music was ever young and grew younger still with advancing years.—What was it that stayed the same as the delicate, almost romantic eighteen-year-old man grew into a stubborn, fiery seventy-five-year-old youth? The rarest thing of all: a blending of the man and the artist. His musical forms recall his thoughts; his motifs resemble his speech. The thinking and the musical structure are equally nontraditional and characteristic; his spoken words and his motifs share the same vitality, eruptive concision, and vehemence. Janáček's music, ripened in the Lachian countryside, recalls the fragrance of that raw rich soil. It is the music of a man who harkens to an inner voice, music vibrant with the most tender sensibility and shaken with racking passion in equal measure.

Janáček created a new Czech style. We need only consider "On an Overgrown Path" as an exemplar of his piano works, the Concertino of his chamber music, the Sinfonietta of his orchestral output, the choral ballad "Maryčka Magdónova" of his vocal music, "Katya Kabanova" of his operas—and these works are only a fraction of Janáček's extensive œuvre. In his *piano music* there is an intimate, unstylized voice which in this day and age of a Richard Strauss-like cacophony suggests the hooting of an owl that will not be flushed out. The *chamber works* mark the transition from a fervently lyrical style, in the two string quartets, to abrupt joyfulness in the sextet "Youth" and dark passion of the "Diary of a Vanished Man," and finally to the characteristic, dramatically explosive expression of the Concertino.

His *vocal works* are based on the folk music of Moravia; and Janáček's transcriptions of folk songs are invaluable on historic grounds alone.

It is in his *orchestral compositions* that one can best discern Janáček's architectonic style. In them he uses neither classic nor romantic principles (indeed, he uses them nowhere); rather, he creates his own characteristic structural style, organically derived from the work by way of the motif. Complexes of small forms arise whose coherence is based on a unique truthfulness of invention rather than on some dominant structural notion. Expansive transformations of the motif take the place of development in a sonata sense. That is also the method in Janáček's most proper domain, in *opera*. The composer is in love with his motif, which he obstinately repeats, diminishes, enlarges, and intensifies in all possible ways; yet he renounces it the moment the spiritual disposition of the characters changes and seeks a new motif more appropriate to the new situation.

That music originating from a synthesis of an awesome temperament and tender dreamfulness, of stormy energy and gentle sensibility, music that finds expression in unrelenting motivistic detail and at the same time in audaciously structured grand forms—that such music produces an effect of the rarest unity—this is the superimaginative achievement of a genius that must conquer the world. One might have forecast from his basic bent that Janáček too would sooner or later consciously close ranks with the innovators. He did it sooner rather than later, and became one of the most audacious of them. His way of taking hold of the material, his subjective but truthful creative activity was destined to become a model for the entire young generation.

2

The unique spontaneity of Janáček's musical vocabulary has been appraised more than once in these pages. Let us add only that the composer's genius has enabled him to resolve the problem of *pianistic style* with the same assurance with which he approached the cardinal problems of dramatic creation. His immense wealth of melodic invention is conveyed in the most trifling phrase. The range of eloquence extends from the description of the softest step On an Overgrown Path to the stormily dramatic expression of raging elements in the composer's spiritual landscape and melts into the translucent yet opaque mist of the outer world.

"Over the mounts of pain went the heart," over still acres where all that is ever heard is an owl's hooting, where a deep-seated longing is somehow rooted—to burst into a dance, here of all places, on this melancholy plain, a longing that grows overpowering and yet must be overcome: a boundless pain seizes the throat—the owl has not flown, not yet, and will never, never fly.

That is Janáček's world, so often sunless, enveloped in mist, and sad enough to make one weep. Yet how that world can change and brighten the instant the sun breaks through and lights up everything with all its force! In the first part of the cycle "In the Mists" there is such a moment. It is as if a group of yeomen had looked up from their labor for a spell to cry out for joy.—And then there are days that are *all* brightness, hallowed by the divine hush of nature; elsewhere yearning and passion flay the soul, there all breaks out in a joyful lively dance, and then again the tragedy and pathos of death intrude. "Here fell the bloodstained simple workman František Pavlík. . . . He came only to voice his zeal for higher learning and was cut down by brutal murderers" (1. X. 1905).

All, all that is human burned in Janáček's innermost being; the only thing he never did was to grow old. It is a fiery youngster who after fifty years of composing can write the Concertino, a piece whose epigraph might have been, Forward, ever forward!

Janáček's pianistic expressivity was as manifold as his inner life. All gradations of pianistic expression are represented—from the simplest melodic phrase, proffered with a native nobility, to the severely dramatic manifestation in the form of a solid piano movement. Few masters of classic and romantic piano music have produced works in which purposeful technique joins with purely musical values in so perfect a synthesis as Janáček achieved. Here a trill is not a pianistic plaything, it is a piece of melody. Runs have their melodic articulation. Rhythm is not dictated by dry calculation but by the beat of an ecstatic heart. Each movement has its own countenance, a personal singularity that is truly unforgettable.

MAIN SOURCES

In addition to the works listed below, the author has consulted dozens of publications about and by Janáček and Brod, as well as several people who knew one or both: Peter Herman Adler and Rudolf Firkušný (New York), William Ritter's adopted son Josef Ritter-Tscherf (Morcote, Switzerland), and Brod's nephew Francis Sterne (Sheffield). Rudolf Firkušný read the entire manuscript, as did his wife Taťána Firkušná, Sir Charles Mackerras, Francis Sterne, and John Tyrrell; all made valuable suggestions for its improvement, especially Dr. Tyrrell. Thanks for providing additional information and materials are due to Jarmil Burghauser (Prague), Nicholas John (English National Opera, London), George Korngold (North Hollywood, California), Jan Kundera (Paris), Jaroslav Mráček (San Diego State University), Janis Susskind (London), and Robert Tuggle (Metropolitan Opera, New York).

Of the several dozen works consulted, the following proved to be most relevant:

Max Brod, *Leoš Janáček: Leben und Werk,* Vienna: Philharmonischer Verlag, 1925.

Max Brod, *Sternenhimmel: Musik- und Theatererlebnisse,* Prague: Orbis, and Munich: Kurt Wolff, 1923.

Max Brod, *Streitbares Leben,* Munich: Kindler, 1960, and Herbig, 1969.

Hugo Gold, ed., *Max Brod: Ein Gedenkbuch, 1884–1968,* Tel Aviv: Olemanu, 1969.

Vladimír Helfert, *Leoš Janáček: V poutech tradice,* Brno: Pazdírek, 1939.

František Kožík, *Po zarostlém chodníčku: Zblížení s Leošem Janáčkem,* Prague: Československý spisovatel, 1967.

Jan Racek and Artuš Rektorys, eds., *Korespondence Leoše Janáčka s Maxem Brodem,* Prague: Státní nakladateltsví krásné literatury, hudby a umění, 1953 (vol. 9 of the Janáček Archive series); also vol. 6 (correspondence with Gabriela Horvátová, 1950) and vol. 8 (correspondence with Marie Calma and Dr. František Veselý, 1951).

Ivo Stolařík, *Jan Löwenbach a Leoš Janáček: Vzájemná korespondence,* Opava: Slezský studijní ústav, 1958.

John Tyrrell, "Janáček, Leoš," in *The New Grove Dictionary of Music and Musicians,* ed. Stanley Sadie, London: Macmillan Publishers, 1980, vol. 9, pp. 474–490.

Jaroslav Vogel, *Leoš Janáček: Život a dílo,* Prague: Státní hudební nakladatelství, 1963.

Berndt W. Wessling, *Max Brod: Ein Portrait,* Stuttgart: Kohlhammer, 1969.

Biobibliographical Name Index